Waterscapes

Planning, Building and Designing with Water

# WATERSCAPES

Edited by
Herbert Dreiseitl
Dieter Grau
Karl H.C. Ludwig

Birkhäuser
Basel · Berlin · Boston

# Contents

Preface . . . . . . . . . . . . . . . . . . . . . . . . . 9

Robert Woodward: **Water in landscape** . . . . . . . . . . 12

Town hall square, Hattersheim . . . . . . . . . . . . . . 14
Water features in an hotel foyer near Neuchâtel . . . . . . 20
Watercourse at Herne-Sodingen Academy . . . . . . . . . 22
The new town square in Gummersbach . . . . . . . . . . 28
The new centre in Kogarah near Sydney . . . . . . . . . . 34
Open space for a residential development in Ittigen, Berne 36

Herbert Dreiseitl: **Water is universal** . . . . . . . . . . . . 40

The water system in Berlin's Potsdamer Platz . . . . . . . . 44
The climate in the Nuremberg Prisma . . . . . . . . . . . . 50
Wind- and water-wheel in Owingen . . . . . . . . . . . . . 56
Solar City Linz . . . . . . . . . . . . . . . . . . . . . . . . 58
Rainwater for the bears in Zurich zoo . . . . . . . . . . . 62
Sonnenhausen estate in Glonn . . . . . . . . . . . . . . . 66
Bathing-pond near Salzburg . . . . . . . . . . . . . . . . . 68
Rainwater management in Coffee Creek, Indiana, USA . . . 70

Wolfgang F. Geiger: **Think global, act local** . . . . . . . . 72

Rainwater retention on the Kronsberg in Hanover . . . . . 76
The Scharnhauser Park in Ostfildern . . . . . . . . . . . . 80
Living in the Backum valley in Herten . . . . . . . . . . . . 84
Sewage treatment plant at the Wörme Hofgemeinschaft in
Handeloh . . . . . . . . . . . . . . . . . . . . . . . . . . . 88
Scheme for the banks of the Volme, Hagen . . . . . . . . . 92
Green roof for Chicago City Hall . . . . . . . . . . . . . . . 96
The Lanferbach at Schüngelberg estate in Gelsenkirchen . 98
Housing estate in Echallens near Lausanne . . . . . . . . 102
Rainwater management in Krems Business Park, Austria . 104

Wolfram Schwenk: **Water as an open system** . . . . . . . 106

Water phenomena in the Gelsenkirchen cooling tower . . 108
Healing garden in Königsfeld . . . . . . . . . . . . . . . . 112
Fountain sculpture in Immenstaad . . . . . . . . . . . . . 114
documenta urbana Kassel . . . . . . . . . . . . . . . . . . 118
»Dunsthöhle« and main avenue in Bad Pyrmont . . . . . 120

Detlev Ipsen: **Towards a new water culture** . . . . . . . 124

»Water-traces« in Hannoversch Münden . . . . . . . . . 128
Interior courtyard of an old people's home in Stuttgart . . 132
Schafbrühl housing estate, Tübingen . . . . . . . . . . . 136
A fountain for the blind in Ulm . . . . . . . . . . . . . . . 138
Water playground in Pforzheim . . . . . . . . . . . . . . . 140

Dieter Grau, Alexander Edel, Gerhard Hauber,
Herbert Dreiseitl:
**From the idea to the finished object** . . . . . . . . . . . 144

Technical data . . . . . . . . . . . . . . . . . . . . . . . . 156
List of works . . . . . . . . . . . . . . . . . . . . . . . . . 160
The authors . . . . . . . . . . . . . . . . . . . . . . . . . 174
Illustration credits . . . . . . . . . . . . . . . . . . . . . . 175

# Preface

»Take thought, when you are speaking of water, that you first recount your experiences, and only afterwards your reflections.«

This piece of advice comes from no less a source than Leonardo da Vinci. But which of us could say that we have experienced water sensually in all its dimensions, to say nothing of understanding it intellectually?

Experience is the starting-point for this book. Experiencing water in nature, and surprises derived from conducting experiments in a water studio, finally led to the water features placed between people and their surroundings that are shown here. Because they make a contribution to townscapes or landscapes we have called them »waterscapes«. Twenty years ago, when I started working with water in public spaces in towns and on housing estates, my first projects were fountains designed for squares in towns and country communities. However satisfying this kind of experience may be for a sculptor, it left me with a feeling of unease. I was particularly dissatisfied with one very common idea: water as a decoration in the townscape, a pleasant toy for artists and architects, but a superfluous one sometimes – and this is said while all the essential water management in the town, like for example rainwater removal, drinking water provision and sewage disposal, is dealt with functionally, scarcely visibly and without any aesthetic sense as part of the engineers' domain.

So on the one hand we have water as a sporadic superficial embellishment for all and on the other hand functional municipal water management, accessible and comprehensible only to specialists. And public awareness of this topic seemed to me to be similarly split, whereas in future we should be increasingly concerned with being able to experience water and gain insights into how to handle it sustainably. Because without this insight, priorities in society and politics will be too weak to preserve this resource in sufficient quality and quantity, while it is of existential importance for evolution and for future generations.

This experience quickly led to ideas about linking water-art with more complex themes: new and more visible routes for rainwater to avoid floods, comprehensible re-use as service water or newly designed approaches for more natural sewage treatment. I am also interested in human-aesthetic and social aspects. This led to a deliberate qualitative change in ambient and urban sounds with images created by the sound of water, or to light presentations using water, down to the air-conditioning of rooms and, just as importantly for people, to adventure areas, water playgrounds, art installations and to workshops and projects aimed at citizen participation.

From the outset the key to our professional approach and to the studio concept was working in an interdisciplinary team. Over the years, we brought experts together who were keen to go beyond their own specialist training as architects, engineers or designers and get to know other people's ideas and subjects, and thus become overall artists in a team dealing with water in all its aspects. Through our work we have jointly met major specialists who are now our friends, and some of them have made a central contribution to this book as authors. They have written in essay form and each of them presents a view that is entirely its own. Here the sum is greater than the parts, and also the result of interdisciplinary work.

This book is written against the background of practice, and hopes to speak in the spirit of the opening quotation. The numerous examples of our work together, which has now extended over 20 years, are intended to be the principal source for illustrating this idea; they are arranged in groups relating to the essays. We look back on all this experience and these working processes with great gratitude, but this is owed above all to the people who made this possible for us.

As the people responsible for putting the book together, we were amazed by the diversity of everything that emerged. Dieter Grau was responsible for general organization and supervision, Karl Ludwig contributed experience and advice, and my role was to provide the concept for the book.

We would like to thank our authors and friends for their expert work and patience in co-ordinating the essays: Professor Wolfgang Geiger, Professor Detlev Ipsen, Wolfram Schwenk, Robert Woodward and not least my colleagues in the Dreiseitl studio.

We were able to secure the services of Stefan Leppert for the project texts and also for editorial work on the essays. We owe this rewarding co-operation a large number of stimulating ideas. Michael Kimmerle dealt with layout and graphics in a masterly fashion. Not least, we would like to thank our publishers, and here we are particularly grateful to Ria Stein, who has worked with us and advised us most attentively, and edited the text as a whole.

Herbert Dreiseitl

# Water in landscape

**Robert Woodward**

**Water is not just a vital element in our lives, it can also be experienced in a whole variety of ways. It creates different kinds of atmosphere and moods that appeal to our feelings.**

Water is a universal landscape element. It is the vital element which can bring life to any landscape; immediate life, constant life. Water's wonderful contribution to this world has been to shape the hard landscape through its immense forces of erosion and to create the soft landscape through its gentle nurture of vegetation.

In itself it is the fundamental soft element. It is a sculptural medium unsurpassed in its potential to make the most of its form, transparency, reflectivity, refractivity, colour, movement and sound. It is a most desirable medium for a landscape designer. But such bounty is not gratuitous. It demands knowledge and understanding for effective use.

Knowledge can be acquired through study, both theoretical and practical.

There is an abundance of theoretical knowledge available. Most of this is for industrial, civil or naval application and thus has little direct relevance to water as a landscape element. While it may be of little use in creative design, however, it is of utmost value in analysing how interesting water effects occur. Knowledge is necessary to be able to incorporate such water effects in design concepts and to sustain them in finished works.

Practical knowledge comes from experience acquired through observation, photography, sketches, written description and physical contact. The physics of ripples are demonstrated by the appearance and disappearance of fine silvery texture on the water surface which can be seen when a zephyr brushes a still lake. The forces inherent in the motion of large waves can be felt by swimmers. The circular pull up and down, and to and fro, can be felt by standing still in the swell of passing waves.

Understanding comes from knowledge, through thought and an open mind.

Fountains are usually created as a response to a design brief which includes the client's budget, time limitations, desired life, durability, maintenance availability, water supply and, especially, the chosen site. The site can be a rich complex of properties of space, scale, climate, existing environment, character and people's activities. These can be seen as constraints or can be thankfully accepted as opportunities by a creative designer. Knowledge and understanding of water and sensitive appreciation of its character are helpful with these projects.

Water can create an atmosphere which stirs almost any emotion.

In nature many factors contribute to the character of water:

**Setting** Consider a bronze bowl brimming with water. How it would seem on a dry dusty desert plain as compared with immersion in the lush green growth of a rainforest gully? It would conjure up quite different feelings. Think of the same bowl high on a rocky snow covered mountain, in a city surrounded by tall buildings or in a suburban garden.

**Containment** Effects vary with the containment of the water body. Open expansive freedom when edged by a gradually shelving sandy beach. Restriction between high rock walls in a river gorge. Scattered, hardly defined at all, almost lost among the reeds of a swamp. Globules of dew, shaped by surface tension, on a soft green leaf. Wetted surface of pavement, free of binding surface tension.

**Movement** Water is never more beautiful than when it is still. Motionless, a small pond or a vast ocean instils a sense of peace of mind. The tranquility of water is conveyed to anyone who cares to stop. Steady gravity flow in rivers and canals or currents from tides in the sea, cause surface undulations or swell. This gentle activation of the water surface conveys a related mood change in people. The feeling varies according to the water mass and velocity of the lazy-smooth or writhing-sensuous undulations.

The description »blackwater« applies when the surface is unbroken, no matter how active or massive the movement. This is an apt term to be applied because the water itself can hardly be seen. When the surface is broken, air bubbles are taken in. These bubbles form a multitude of spheres which reflect light and so make the water much more visible, especially in depth. This is called »whitewater«: cascades, waterfalls, tzunamis.

**Lighting** In the dark, the presence of water may be sensed by sound or smell. Even when it cannot be seen, its presence is felt. It is not always necessary to light water. Sometimes the gentlest light from the moon accentuates mysticism. This is so when the smooth sensuous surface of oozing blackwater is highlighted by bright reflected images of the moon. This beauty owes a debt to the small, relatively intense light source. The effect of disbursed, low intensity, light from a dull winter sky on an exposed stretch of water may make people feel more depressed and even cold because that is how the water appears.

Man made water elements are often best lit by existing area lighting which makes them coherent with the environment. Sunlight is desirable when water action and excitement are to be maximized. The brilliance of sunlight shows as sparkle on reflective surfaces, illuminates each curvatious bubble and penetrates clear water to show pool bottoms or make moving wave shadows. A mixture of sun and shade gives complexity and introduces time to the equation by varying effects as the sun's position changes from sunrise to sunset. Lighting utilizes the optical qualities of water's transparency with reflection and refraction. Artificial lighting can create new expressions by free choice of light sources.

**Wind** Streams flow regularly unless loaded by heavy rain, tides follow a consistent pattern unless disturbed by major earth movement, but wind changes dramatically season by season, day by day or even moment by moment.

Motionless air at the surface leaves water completely smooth like a mirror. The gentlest air flow is usually light puffs which brush the surface and disturb patches of the mirror intermittently. Air does not flow at a constant speed at the earth's surface because friction against land or water causes turbulence, even at very low velocities. At more than a few kilometres per hour there is enough energy conveyed to create surface ripples. These are very small waves of up to ten centimetres wavelength which are called surface tension waves. They appear in an instant and can disappear just as quickly because the surface tension of the flat mirror can dominate and so kill them. Stronger winds blow up larger gravity waves. These are quite different in action as they have acquired enough energy from the wind to be able to continue for a long distance.

Gravity waves are rather like sound waves. They move in a constant direction until they gradually lose their energy, are impeded by an obstruction or are reflected from a solid surface. Reflected or refracted waves move back through primary waves and form interference patterns; absolutely fascinating and often beautiful. Constantly blowing wind increases the height and wavelength until monstrous waves, which can travel thousands of kilometres, develop. Winds are created by the earth's pressure gradients and temperature differential. Their turbulence is influenced by physical barriers. Wind blows water from jets and waterfalls to form spray.

**Sound** Sound is nature's most delightful way to herald the presence of water. The mellow rumble of the ocean, out of site beyond sand dunes or the gentle gurgle of a trout stream foretells what is ahead.

Water's sounds have all the characteristics of music; variety of volume and pitch, sharpness, softness, rhythm and, most importantly, harmony. Falling water in cascades is heard as a range of superimposed frequencies. The pitch and character of each sound depends on the mass of individual water units and landing surface. Massive bulk flow to almost weightless droplets fall a variety of distances and land in deep water, shallow water or even on bare rock and generate a multitude of sounds.

Raindrops produce different sounds on roof iron, sand or stone pavement. The level of sound from water can vary from absolute silence to a numbing volume.

**Colour** Water in nature is rarely a »colourless liquid« as the dictionary says. Often water is tinged with vegetative stains or coloured with suspended clay. This clay being opaque particles, affects turbidity so much that a shadow cast on the surface can be as sharp as if it was cast on mud.

Most colour we see in water is either from surroundings reflected on the surface or underwater objects seen through its transparent body. The degree to which we see reflected colours depends on the angle of viewing due to the refraction angles between air and water (hence a fisherman's efforts to keep low and so remain unseen by his quarry) and light differential. A sunlit red and white building is easily reflected on the surface of a pool which has a dark bottom.

**Depth** »The deep blue« The deeper the water the deeper its colour. A view of a coral atoll from the air is remarkable for the wonderful variation of tones in blues and greens in the surrounding seas. Light is absorbed as it passes through the transparent medium. Any colour from the light source, which is often the clear blue sky, gets deeper and deeper as the light intensity reduces with depth.

The joy of effectively working with water, by knowing and understanding the medium, is the reward for study and diligence. It is the same sort of joy that a blacksmith gets from forging cherry red iron and cabinet maker from paring sweet smelling rosewood.

# Town hall square, Hattersheim

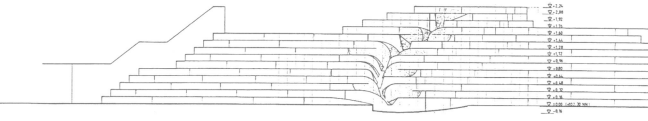

Elevation of the steps and
the projected water cascade

Form modelling with a 1:1
model, built and tested with
water in the workshop

The individual elements
are placed and assembled
to the precise millimetre.
Each stone is hand-crafted
and produced individually.

On the route from A to B our attention is usually caught by the destination. The space in between becomes a side issue. In town planning the familiar phrase »the route is the destination« became a platitude amidst all the enthusiasm for building and refurbishment. It was only in the mid-eighties that towns started to try to atone for their sins committed in the post-war period by transforming open space from being an area that had to be bridged into a space offering a whole range of different potential experiences.

This has been brought off successfully in Hattersheim. This little town has excellent transport links with various autobahns and local railways, and is close to the airport, and so has become a desirable and highly prosperous industrial location within the belt south of Frankfurt. But developments of this kind rarely turn out positively for the town's appearance – even though communities are increasingly aware that they compete with each other and have to offer their residents attractive urban spaces. Hattersheim found itself facing this challenge in the late eighties. The community focused its attention on the town centre and announced a competition for developing the area between the town hall and the municipal park. This was a marketplace, and they wanted it to develop a life of its own, forming a link between urban and rural elements: the town hall was intended to draw people, restaurants would be able to use attractive spaces in the open air, the route to the adjacent park would make people want to linger there, and also provide a new way of getting into the park itself. Water became the linking element in the Hattersheim marketplace. The steps leading to the town hall are the heart of the ensemble and the source of the water. An inviting or at least alluring gesture was successfully provided by a water cascade made up of flowform

The flowing water
intertwines with
the marketplace.
Cafés and shops
use the area as
a foyer.

basins. Herbert Dreiseitl had the basins cut to the millimetre from granite blocks, after developing and testing the movement of the water in his studio in clay and plaster models on a scale of 1:1. The slightest departure from the ideal form would mean that the water would not run as wished in its figure-of-eight pattern based on John Wilkes' flow principle, which is intended to be reminiscent of a human pulse.

From the lowest step, the water falls on to the granite paving of the marketplace, runs under two five-metre squares and then reappears in brick basins. It then becomes a plaything, with a straight brick edge on the market place side and a curved one on the catering side, broken up with blocks of stone.

The water pulsates its way gradually from step to step, falling into a specially cast outlet.

Plan of the marketplace showing the steps and watercourse.

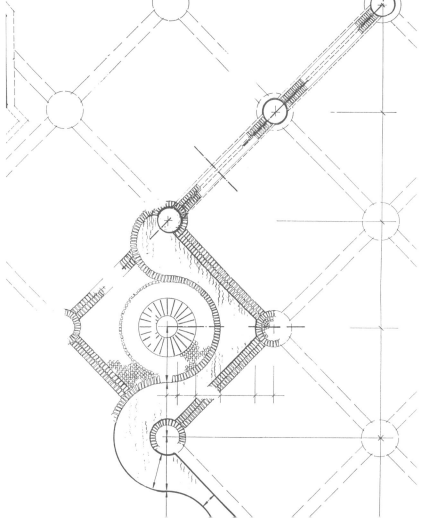

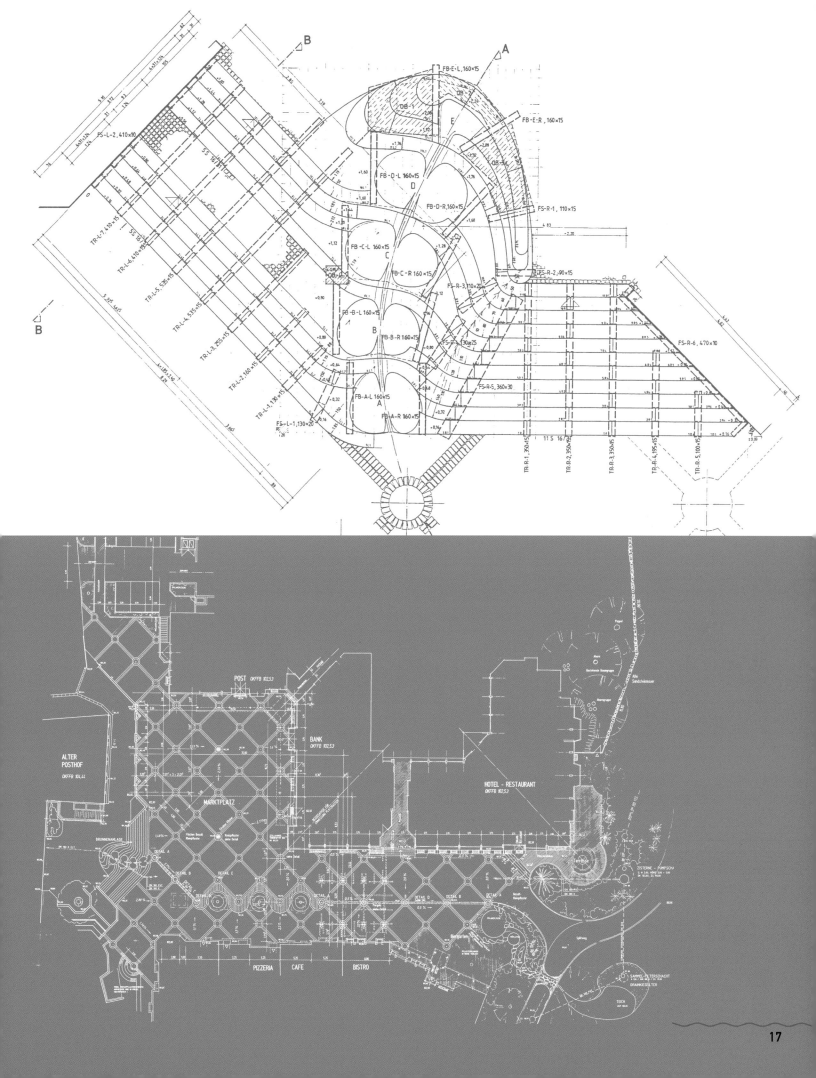

Towards the pond, the watercourse is planted and more natural in appearance.

Here the water plunges under the paving again to re-emerge at the end of the pedestrian area in a planted pool. There it is cleaned and taken through an open ford into a pond on the edge of the park. It then runs underground to a tank, and is pumped back up to the source on the town hall steps. A way from the town hall to the park has become a way of taking people to water.

Water remains visible and enters into a playful dialogue with the path at a crossing.

The water meanders gently through the park to the pond.

The pond in the park is used for water retention.

The stream runs through a purification biotope into the aerated retention pool.

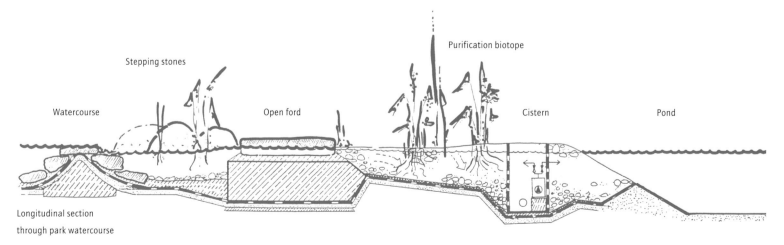

Longitudinal section through park watercourse

# Water features in an hotel foyer near Neuchâtel

Spring water from the hill-side trickles over a block of natural stone. It seeps through planted pools before flowing into the hotel foyer.

Here you can hear water – a musical fountain enlivens the foyer of an hotel in the Swiss Jura.

Cups are mounted off centre striking the long bronze rods as they are filled and tip over. This produces ground tones with harmonic series, and the bass notes are reinforced by resonating plates set on fine bearings.

The musical fountain with trickling water forms the central focus of the hotel complex foyer.

Water runs through metal channels and down to thin metal chains where it collects in small cups. These then tip over when they are full.

Water is scarce in karstic areas. And this is also the case in Montézillon, a small town above Neuchâtel in the Swiss Jura. This is where the L'Aubier hotel and restaurant and its adjacent farm-land and sales outlet are to be found, with a panoramic view over central Switzerland as far as the Alps. The old auberge and the buildings in the court-yard were rebuilt from the foundations a few years ago and have been run on modern environmental technology ever since – this extends from solar hay dry-ing and an integrated combined heat and power plant to using rainwater for all the toilets and washing and cleaning facilities.

The whole of the immediate vicinity was redesigned along with the build-ings. A new garden in which the typical Jura landscape is presented on a small scale was created between the hotel-restaurant, which was brought up to date and extended by a new wing on one side, and the working farmstead with its more functionally designed buildings and land on the other. In addition to this, a new feature of this ensemble of landscape and buildings was water – which is a rarity in this karstic region, and thus seems all the more valuable.

The first step towards creating the water features is that drainage and spring water is collected on the upper part of the sloping site. It then gushes visibly out of a large block of natural stone whose surface has been polished to mirror smoothness. Following the meandering structure of the veins in the stone, which were sand-blasted and deepened for this purpose, the water trickles into geometrical pools contai-ning aquatic plants. The pools are part of a staircase that is the main access point to the new foyer between the hotel and the restaurant. From here the water flows via an open channel in the paving and an opening in the glass wall (submerged wall) into the two-storey foyer. There it flows via two channels built into the floor covering of the main floor that lead to the foyer parapet and jut out beyond it a little. The lower level of the foyer is a good three metres below; the fall from this height via a sound-producing system in which the water becomes a musician in its own right is the creative climax of the water-course.

To produce this effect, the water slips down fine chains and runs into cups that are suspended so that they can move; once they are full, they tip over. As they empty, cup and chain start to move like a pendulum and strike against twelve long bronze rods that stand freely in the space like a sculpture. Different rods are struck apparently at random. The hard-ened bronze rods, which are up to six metres long, start to vibrate, thus pro-ducing floating ground-notes across the full range of the harmonic series. Heavy metal sheets mounted on the floor so that they can vibrate reinforce the reso-nance of the deep notes and combine with the sound of the bubbling, dripping water to form sound patterns reminis-cent of the music of the spheres. The water collects in a pool and slides from there via channels into another planted pool and then finally leaves the building again via a second submerged wall.

Numerous models were needed, as well as sketches, in the planning and construction phases of this water fea-ture. The musical fountain alone called for a large number of experiments with water on a scale of 1:1; the composer Heiner Ruhland also helped with the tuning. But visitors and residents scarcely take any notice of that or of the many fiddly technical details: they are simply fascinated by the sound, the light effects and the originality of the whole feature, which extends over three storeys and constantly offers new aspects from different points of view.

# Watercourse at Herne-Sodingen Academy

The Emscher Park International Building Exhibition was held between 1989 and 1999, in an area bounded by Kamen in the east and Duisburg in the west, Recklinghausen in the north and Essen in the south. It was also a ten-year celebration of structural change in Europe's largest industrialized area. This entire region in the heart of Germany was celebrated as an incomplete work of art that will in fact never be finished. Birches and poplars climb up the peaceful slag-heaps. Most of the pit-head gear has come to a standstill, and only a very few of the chimneys are still belching smoke. Printed circuit boards for computers are soldered here now, and scarcely any steel girders are welded. The acclaimed Emscher Park IBA ended on 1 October 1999. And the closing ceremony was held in a place that could not be more futuristic and that could not show the structural change to a service society more vividly: it was at the Education Academy in Herne-Sodingen of the Ministry for Home Affairs. Coal had been mined here from 1871 to 1978, and thirty hectares of contaminated land left behind, and now several buildings stand under a single roof. People come out of the buildings, but they remain under cover and behind glass.

A rectangular pool of water thrusts out from under this glass into the forecourt. From there a man-made »Fissure« races via four plinths and flights of steps in the direction of one of the abandoned shafts of the Mont Cenis pit. Cracks in the surface of the earth are commonplace in this coal-bearing region, which is characterized by mining subsidence, but this one is different – it has water flowing in it. The watercourse is contained by rough steel shuttering, sealed with strips of plastic and concrete and covered with gravel. It turns several sharp corners, and opens up a little in some places. Triangular pieces of metal are welded to the bed on the steps,

A fissure runs through the forecourt of the Mont Cenis Education Adademy. It suggests faults and subsidence caused by the mining here, and indeed, throughout the Ruhr region.

The hard structural language of the installation and the use of steel, water and rust produces a distinct aesthetic.

The Academy interior: the use of water within the climate envelope creates a Mediterranean atmosphere.

Water cascades on the terraces show interesting flow phenomena, developed in experiments in the workshop.

Plan showing the water fissure and academy pools

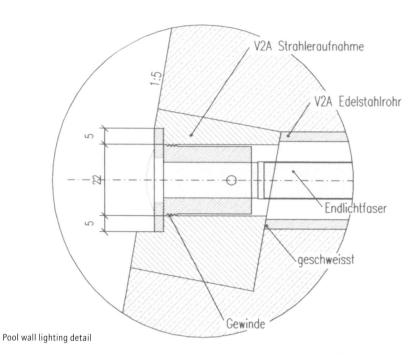

V2A Strahleraufnahme

V2A Edelstahlrohr

1:5

Endlichtfaser

geschweisst

Gewinde

Pool wall lighting detail

Section through a water outlet

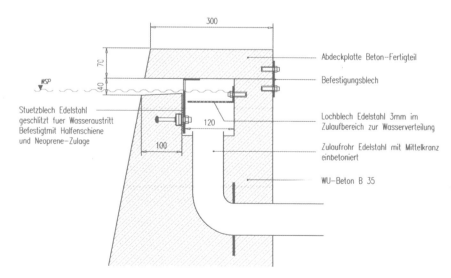

Abdeckplatte Beton-Fertigteil

Befestigungsblech

Stuetzblech Edelstahl geschlitzt fuer Wasseraustritt Befestigtmit Halfenschiene und Neoprene-Zulage

Lochblech Edelstahl 3mm im Zulaufbereich zur Wasserverteilung

Zulaufrohr Edelstahl mit Mittelkranz einbetoniert

WU-Beton B 35

300

70

40

120

100

WSP

forming obstacles that produce interesting currents. The watercourse ends in the »Depths«, a triangular pool in which the water only seems to seep away. In fact 40 centimetres of water remain in it, and the water that flows in is pumped back from here to the pools in the Academy building. Herbert Dreiseitl sees these »Depths« as a sculpture, rather than as a working pool of water. On one side visitors stand above the »Depths«, behind a barrier to prevent them falling made up of crude steel sheets three millimetres thick. The water falls one metre down from the channel into the pool under their feet. Opposite, rusty sheets of metal are placed on a metal plinth, arranged apparently randomly as steps. This is not a place for sitting down, but more a place for looking, for remembering the region's iron and steel days. Floodlights mounted under the sheets forming the steps plunge the »Depths« into a mysterious light after dark. The »Fissure« also makes a more powerful effect at night because it is lit. Water vapour emerges from illuminated chinks, an illusion to the underground mining activities that used to take place here.

As in numerous IBA projects, the »Fissure« and the »Depths« are intended to symbolize the transition from one epoch to another.

The water fissure under construction, showing the steel structure of the foundations. The Academy is in the background, with the largest solar roof in Europe.

The water disappears down into the depths.

A flow phenomenon detail at a slight change in level in the cascade – here the water starts to pulsate.

# The new town square in Gummersbach

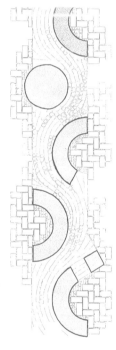

Plan and detail view of
the sculpted installations.

Gummersbach is the chief town of its district, Oberberg, which it runs with creditable efficiency: the economy flourishes. The prosperity of this town of 50,000 inhabitants 50 kilometres east of Cologne has been on a solid basis from time immemorial. A small-scale, balanced mixture of industry, trade, agriculture and services has always produced – to express it positively – self-confident people. But this had unfortunate consequences for the central Lindenplatz in the sixties. In an act of bold self-overestimation, examples of medieval timber-frames, classicism and Jugendstil were all pulled down and replaced with dreary progressive buildings completely surrounded by concrete slabs, everything grey on grey. And life gradually disappeared from the town centre. Now the town wants to get away from the dreary image conveyed by these buildings without any sense of scale, style or category, but they are not as easily pulled down as their predecessors. And so in the mid-nineties people concentrated all the more on the squares and walkways in the pedestrian area. And because a large number of individuals have an interest in these areas in particular, representatives from the local authority, the residents and the service and retail industries were invited to a discussion about new design ideas. The participants in the discussion quickly agreed on a modern water landscape. Symbolically this was seen to stand for movement, and possibly also change, uniqueness and something that was most convincing of all for the people of Gummersbach: a place where people would come to meet each other again. And they do.

One place that appeals, for example, is by the spring, with its fan-shaped, sculpted natural stone slabs, with lights between them to create mysterious areas of light and shade in the twilight. From there the water flows down a slight slope through a curved channel

Hands and feet can be used to touch and grasp water structures and currents – an experience for all the senses, and for the young and old.

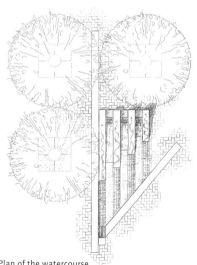

Plan of the watercourse source: Water gushes forth from stone slabs set at different angles.

Carefully designed handling of waves and light transforms an ordinary object into sparkling jewels.

Idea sketch for the new
Lindenplatz, a square in
the town centre, formerly
just a big car park.

The inlaid glass is lit
by fibre optics.

towards Lindenplatz, guided by round
prefabricated concrete units and running over cascades; on the way it disappears briefly underground, to provide
a roadway for delivery traffic and
rhythm to the running water. At the
top of the square the water runs under
an artistically punched-out covering
into a jagged pool walled in natural
stone. Long steps intended for people
to sit on thrust out from the jagged pool
into the square. In the pool the water
flows over a surface that is designed
with great variety, with little mounted
bronze waves, for example, or shallow,
curved cascades that create exciting
patterns in the current. Floodlights
plunge the water into a scene that is
strange but made familiar by the
medium of water, in which everything
seems to have water flowing around
it. At the end of this pool the water
is taken back underground to its fan-
shaped source.

Particularly impressive
at night, horizontal and
vertical light structures are
interpreted and reflected
by moving water. It has
become a popular attraction
for people.

The main entrance to the
Sparkasse bank in Linden-
platz is accented by a 15
metres high light, glass
and water sculpture. The
horizontal, glowing lines
of inlaid glass appear in
vertical form here and blend
into the space beyond the
dimensions of the building.

The local savings bank is an immediate neighbour, and has taken up the
water theme separately itself. A unique
line of water made up of glowing, coloured inlaid glass and built into the
floor covering links the wave pattern in
the pool with a water-and-glass object
in the façade extending over four
storeys. As in the Nuremberg »Prism«
building, Herbert Dreiseitl commissioned the Dierig glass design workshop
to melt several layers of colour into a
flowing form, producing an unframed,
self-supported sheet of glass. Water
falls between two sheets of glass from
a height of 4.5 metres into a planted
pool of water in the entrance area,
drawing in air from the outside through
a slit as it does so, thus providing an
air-conditioning effect. This gives the
square its second landmark.

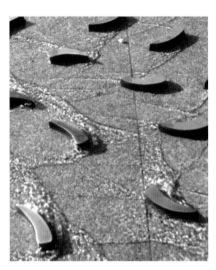

A fluid ribbon full of contrasts between hard and soft, crystalline and organic, running through Gummersbach town centre.

# The new centre in Kogarah near Sydney

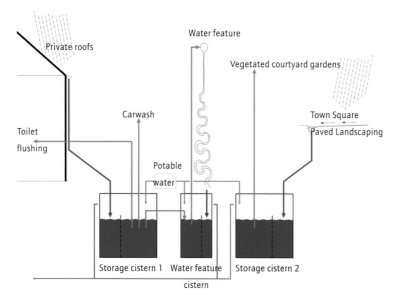

Private roofs

Water feature

Vegetated courtyard gardens

Carwash

Town Square

Paved Landscaping

Toilet flushing

Potable water

Storage cistern 1    Water feature cistern    Storage cistern 2

An innovative water concept makes full use of rainwater collected from the square and roofs. Run-off from the square is used to irrigate the planted inner courtyards.

In Kogarah, a small town near Sydney, the town centre is being redeveloped around the library. An innovative water concept is at the core of the redevelopment.

Experiencing water, discovering phenomena and simply playing make the running water in the middle of the square a dynamic and fun experience for children.

Three capital letters dominated the planning phase for the Sydney Olympics: ESD. And these games will go into history because of ESD – and of course the immensely imaginative opening ceremony. But while the opening ceremony and many fantastic records will survive only as memories, Ecologically Sustainable Development will have a lasting influence on life in the suburb of Homebush Bay. Targets were achieved in terms of energy, water, air, refuse and nature conservancy that will put all future Olympic cities under pressure to take action.

But urban and regional development is being approached on an ESD basis in the city itself as well – at least in some areas. One crucial aspect is water management. Even though the climate is temperate on the east and south-east coastal strips, the Australians are careful about this costly resource here as well: there are millions of people crowded into Melbourne, Canberra and Brisbane. And indeed in Sydney, which is a small town of 60,000 inhabitants but has 36 municipalities that have come within its borders, making it a major city with three and a half million inhabitants. This also includes Kogarah, a typical product of the suburbanization process, without a centre around which life can develop.

The town now intends to build this centre with a wide range of useful buildings and a town square that will follow the principles of the Olympic site on a smaller scale. High-level cultural, economic and environmental goals merge in an integrated planning system. For water management this means: 85 % of the annual precipitation is collected in underground tanks, separated into more heavily soiled water from the new town square and relatively clean water from the roofs. Two thirds of this are used for toilet flushing and a new carwash, and one third for watering green areas and to produce an artificial watercourse. The remaining 15 per cent remain in roof gardens and on terraces. Kogarah thus saves 17 per cent of overall water consumption in comparison with traditional concepts and also reduces peak demand. The running water in the square is designed as a meeting-place – where water can be experienced as an aesthetically valuable resource, rather than as something merely functional.

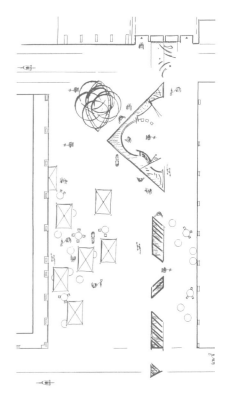

# Open space for a residential development in Ittigen, Berne

Water dancing in air and sun

Plan showing central
fountain and overall
water concept

Revolutionary concepts for housing estates are a thing of the past. Outstanding examples of co-operative housing estate design, in which architecture and the planning of open space complemented each other in graceful moderation, are now listed monuments. Building firms operate on different premises from those of a hundred years ago. But the desire for community, for contact between residents, is still the same as ever.

A bronze sculpture in the Berne »Im Park« estate is an impressive confirmation of this. It stands at the centre of a paved circle in a round pool 25 metres in diameter, and points up to the light with three columns about five metres high. Water streams and patters playfully over the curved collar from one column to the next, then falls into the pool. When the wind makes the curtains of water into thin veils, the static columns seem to become figures dancing with each other – an image of community.

As in numerous other housing estates, open space plays a key role in the Ittigen residential park in Berne. Here 700 people go in and out of 222 flats in twelve buildings. They are looking for places where they can get together or play, for points that they can identify in the traffic-free inner courtyard, which covers about 6,000 square metres. The sloping site on the northern periphery of the Swiss capital offered an outstanding opportunity to put collected rainwater through its paces.

The water starts to flow from five source bowls at the highest point of the courtyard, then collects at first in a pool surmounted by large Norway maples. Large stepping stones in limestone from the nearby Bernese Alps accompany the water to this shady, highly authentic source point. Then the water flows down the slope, into gravelled channels. Occasionally a ford passes through these, made of natural stone columns placed

The central piazza of the
housing development
»Im Park« in Bern-Ittigen

Water currents – deflecting
and gliding slopes fascinate
children.

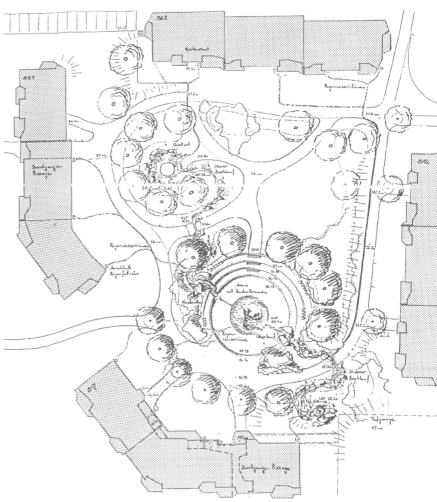

The water sculpture
in winter: the frozen
work of art plays with
the frosty light.

on their sides, and there are also concrete shapes that the water flows
through as gliding and deflecting slopes.
At the edge of the steps leading down
to the so-called arena, curved concrete
channels are built in, and the water
falls from these in a phased rhythm,
flowing on to the fountain sculpture in
a straight line and returning from there
to the source point. If there is a great
deal of rainfall, surplus water passes
from the fountain basin to two ponds
designed to be as close to nature as
possible.

The site has cellars under most of
the area, and gains its dynamic from a
thoughtfully linked network of paths, a
lively topography, from alternating open
spaces and intimate niches, and the
various opportunities to meet others
or to hide, to enjoy the sun or seek out
some shade. But without the subtle
effect of water in the pools, channels,
cascades or fountains the residents
would find it very difficult to identify
this courtyard as something special, as
their own particular habitat with lots
of intriguing sub-habitats. And it is not
until the water in the fountain sculpture
freezes into an icy artwork that the
three columns seem to stand together
properly for the first time, out there in
the freezing cold.

Who is crossing whom?
The water has the same
rights as the path, the
cracks allow for constant
eye contact with the water.

People walking at the
watercourse source.
The source feeds through
five flowforms.

# Water is universal

## Herbert Dreiseitl

**Water is far from being just a designer's resource or a material: it begs to have its vital possibilities rediscovered. This starts at the beginning of the planning process for water projects, and involves linking up and integrating elemental themes. Knowledge of water's particular qualities as a material are needed, and often experiments need to be conducted to give a real idea of the result that will ensue.**

Water is everywhere in our towns, in a labyrinthine system of concealed pipes. It is freely available, and can apparently be disposed of without difficulty. City-dwellers are usually only confronted with it at the various ends of the system in their houses or flats: coming out of the tap into the sink or wash-basin, in the bath or under the shower, with the surge of the flush or when paying the water rates.

But nowadays it is rare to experience water in the open in our towns and cities – and yet it is increasingly in demand. Aesthetically presented and decoratively displayed, from a simple fountain to a showy water installation, it is appreciated as an invigorating element in front of and between the build-ings.

Of course fountains and open waterways in towns and cities are nothing new. There is impressive evidence of them even from ancient times. They give us a sense of how closely urban design has always been linked with water and its use. This functional relationship can be traced from antiquity through the Middle Ages to modern times, and has made a lasting impact on the image of cities. Waterways for goods transport and other traffic, facilities for providing drinking water and removing sewage were crucial when choosing a location and helped to shape the ground plan of a town, the squares and streets. And here water was far more than some-thing that simply had to be supplied and disposed of, it was presented artistically in all the great cultures, emphasized aesthetically and venerated. It created the atmosphere and expressed a living relationship between a town and its sur-rounding area. The way water is handled in towns shows more than the mere technical ingenuity of its citizens, it reflects myth and religion and shows the spiritual constitution of people living in a water culture.

This changed fundamentally during and after the indus-trial revolution: water and waterways were now increasingly brought under control. They were straightened, canalized, built over, buried and even filled in. Trusting entirely to the fact that all this would be technically possible. But this trust was broken by the floods, which came more and more frequently, and with increasing fury.

Now water is one of the key questions as far as the future of our world is concerned, as we have recognized that natu-rally available water supplies are finite, pollution is always just round the corner, and we are aware that water plays a complex role in the stability of eco-systems.

Water is the material basis of man's relationship with his environment, and often stands as a symbol of it. It creates links and is in a state of permanent exchange in relation to warmth, climate, air, soil and gravity. Growth, metabolic change and vital functions are inconceivable without water. Water projects are perhaps so topical because they express a profound longing for life in all its vigour.

Technology and aesthetics are usually kept neatly apart in our brave new urban world as contradictions that cannot be bridged. They often seem to be as far apart as the various pro-fessions and specialist disciplines associated with them – and so the various training courses are neatly separated as well.

### Unknown water

Although we could not survive from day to day without water, we are usually aware of it only superficially and at particular moments. Reduction to simple functions like clean-ing, washing and waste disposal reduces the intricate inter-play of water with our lives to simplified and imprecise images.

Planning and working with water seem simple at first as well – but even the first practical experiences can reveal un-expected and unfathomable depths, and other surprises. For example, water often does not flow in the way that is projec-ted by the computer or on the drawing-board: a curtain of water falls quite differently from the way you anticipated, the desired wave patterns do not materialize, or are not as plan-ned, and the »reflecting pool« you hoped for reflects too rarely – or not at all. And it is also not rare to find that the quality of the water in a newly installed system leaves something to be desired, or a deposit of limescale spoils the look of the expen-sive natural stone basin. Other consequences of such mistaken assessments and ignorance at the planning stage are techni-cal problems and excessively high running costs.

This is not a horror story, but unfortunately it is often the case – and there are a lot of architects, planners, artists and their clients who could tell you a tale about it, and who have foundered on one of these rocks. They then give up, following the motto »once is enough«, or are simply satisfied with going back to banal solutions that have been used all too often in the past.

And there are some places where new fountains and water sculptures can seem out of place or unnatural. This is a sign of approaches that have been worked out in theory, but have nothing to do with the real qualities of water. Indeed there are times when people look at these fountains and sculptures and ask whether it wouldn't have been better to leave the water out altogether. Every artist and planner realizes when designing a water feature that water needs a great deal of respect when you are working with it: it is mysterious, and likes for be investigated sensitively. It is easy to assess when looking at projects and works of art involving water how thoroughly the people planning it understood water. Did the water in the project become a mere side issue, or is this a successful installation that does justice to water and brings out its best qualities? Here at the latest you see whether the planner had real insight, and how sensitively the water has been handled.

## First experience and approaches

The knowledge we acquire at school and from the rest of our education is often not enough to grasp water in all the richness of its many manifestations. You cannot get to the bottom of water with abstractions like chemical and physical formulae, as the ideas associated with them are often too static and distanced. Water is full of dynamism, and it needs a sense of movement in the thinking and ideas of the people dealing with it. Professions that handle water every day gain experience of this kind and know the special inner flexibility that is needed to work with water successfully.

There are all sorts of ways of getting closer to this amazingly flexible material. This includes a number of sports that make it possible to experience water directly and physically, using some quite simple aids: swimming, surfing or diving, to name but three. Sensitive observation of water in a landscape is particularly valuable.

Water and air: You have to start by watching what happens when it rains. The weather front approaches trailing a curtain in the sky, and the threads of rain dance in the wind like a fine veil. If you are lucky, different coloured layers appear in the depths, and sunlight is split into its spectrum in a rainbow. Whether it is a veil of rain, or mist and cloud formations – the images change constantly, influenced by temperature, humidity, air pressure and temperature variations. But water is visible in air only when droplets or ice crystals catch the light.

Surfaces: If droplets fall into a lake from trees on the shore, you see a number of eccentrically expanding rings of waves, that seem to pass through each other without having any effect. Perhaps you can see from stalks, twigs and objects how the waves are diverted there, then break on the shore or are driven back again.

Wave structures with different patterns appear in all places where different media meet, e.g. on the borderline between water and air. Here dimension or scale has only a minor role to play. A fine breath of air, the slightest stimulus is enough to produce an infinite number of rhythmic patterns in a pool or the sea, or even in a little basin. Here again it is worth noticing the play of light, as it is only reflections of the sky, the landscape or of objects that make the wave structures visible to us.

There are planes that appear on borders, and also waves, that are only seldom perceptible. This also includes horizontal interfaces between bodies of water, for example with different densities. These are caused by differences in temperature or different salt contents. We are often aware of them when swimming or diving in summer, and they can oscillate slowly from time to time, as a result of wind, variations in atmospheric pressure etc.

Eddies: A twig blowing in the wind in a lake, stones sticking up out of a stream, the piers of a bridge in a river – the attentive observer will notice a series of eddies produced by all these obstacles. Whole strings of eddies are made visible on the surface by differently reflected light. But most of the eddies in water remain hidden. They are to be found in a large variety of unseen forms, in all waterways. It is not until traces of sand start drifting with the water, or colour is provided by clay or mica-schist, that all this diversity becomes visible.

Meanders: Even small watercourses, like melting glacier water, trails of water trickling over fields of sand below the tongue of a glacier in the mountains, shapes left behind by the falling tide on the beach or glacial valleys that have not been dammed show water's natural tendency to meander.

These examples could continue. A great deal can be observed in nature, but she does impose limits. Random factors caused by a whole range of parameters and conditions that are often unfavourable to precise observation limit perception. And therefore some questions can only be investigated by experiment:

## Experimenting in order to understand water

Even though flow movement in water does follow certain laws, about which we know a great deal today, the specific ways in which they develop are full of surprises. Experiments can be very simple. The more minimal their construction the more astonishing the results often are.

A smooth, water-resistant sheet, as polished as possible, made of something like glass, perspex or wood coated with plastic, is placed in a diagonal position. Water flows on to the highest point of the sheet from a small diameter hose. You expect a thread of water to trickle down in an absolutely straight line, following the shortest possible route according to gravity. And this actually does occur at first. But after a very short time the thread of water changes its course: it starts to swing rhythmically to the right and left, producing a meandering trail of water that changes constantly. Rivulets, streams and rivers form these meanders, leave loops behind and reshape their banks. Entire landscapes are shaped in this way.

Different structures like pools, channels or vessels offer themselves for experiment. Flexible, changeable materials like clay or sand are particularly suitable for studies of this kind. If you wish to determine the inner movements of a body of water, you need to add fine particles or dye. To make surface currents visible you should add lycopodium (club-moss spores), and for three-dimensional movement in water the addition of magnesium dust or a dye like potassium permanganate is recommended. The closer the dye is to the same specific gravity as the liquid, the more clearly the movement can be seen, even when flowing slowly.

### The water workshop: working with real models

It is sensible and advantageous when working out designs with water to work with it in a real form as well. Experience has taught us this: fountain projects, flow details or flow channels that are really interesting and appropriate to water cannot be developed and calculated theoretically, they need experiment, frequently on the scale of one to one.

We are constantly discovering that water is our best teacher. Despite all prior considerations and even with a great deal of experience: water does not always behave as expected. Corrections and constant new experiments are the principal task. The designs improve gradually and start to carry the signature of the water itself.

A water workshop can be simple and robust. In any case it should be well enough equipped to allow a large number of the desired experiments with water to be carried out. It is astonishing how directly and surely water itself holds the mirror up for the designer. In practice we are constantly surprised how immediately convincing ideas can be acquired in this way.

### Linking themes

This is particularly true today: themes involving water are complex and are always directly related to other themes and specialist areas. Isolated water-features that are self-sufficient are no longer in vogue and on close consideration historical fountain complexes always existed in a context of many other functions. They provided drinking and utility water, were a sound instrument for the town, especially at night, and they formed a social focal point where people could meet.

Water themes today: the need for links. Water influences our sense of well-being in towns and in buildings, it affects the humidity, the temperature, the cleanness of the air, the climate. Water can be used in such a way that it filters, cools or warms the outside air and regulates humidity. Experience in the Prisma in Nuremberg or in the Nikolaus-Cusanus-Haus show new ways forward for air-conditioning.

Smell and taste make places unmistakable. It is one of the strongest impressions available if you recognize a town, a location, a season through its smell, and here too water can mediate. The somewhat sickly smell of the haze on a late summer's morning in Venice or the fragrance of blossom by the Seine in Paris in the spring.

The sounds of water against street noise. They are soothing, and compensate for urban stress, never mind the decibel levels. Robert Woodward opened his Opera Café near a busy highway, but surrounded it with a cascade of water, so that you can enjoy your cappuccino in the middle of it, undisturbed and in the best of spirits. And in downtown San Francisco you can escape from the noise of the city and lie down and relax on a lawn by the waterfalls of the Martin Luther King memorial fountain. But even unspectacular small water features can make spaces magical with their special sounds. In the foyer of L'Aubier, a Swiss mountain hotel, a stream of water activates a musical fountain. Water is the artist, the fountain is the musical instrument.

Moving light brings spaces to life. Water distorts, refracts and reflects. It distributes incident light dynamically in connection with its own movement. Working purposefully with light effects and thus using the water surface as an instrument is demonstrated by the examples of urban water in Potsdamer Platz in Berlin, by the finely differentiated waves and watercourses in Gummersbach or the major water scene in Hannoversch Münden. Here the art is to move the water in such a way that it supports the light installation.

Water at the wrong time and in the wrong place causes extra-high tides, floods, erosion and destruction, but also droughts, a lack of groundwater, dried-up aquifers and biotopes, and thus the destruction and elimination of a rich variety of flora and fauna. Water projects have to address creating a balance in water management. Retention, purification, evaporation and infiltration must of course be integral elements in a municipal water programme. Rain retention in the Kronsberg district of Hanover, the green roof to retain and purify rainwater on City Hall in Chicago and the use, storage and integration of water in the new Potsdamer Platz development in central Berlin all count towards this.

And finally, water creates atmosphere, something that is vital to our towns and cities if they are to be individual, unmistakable and easily recognized, with a sense of being home. This is a difficult set of phenomena to describe, and has something to do with the spiritual quality of a place, defining life and movement, which is something that water can convey directly like no other element. Interdisciplinary work and thought are needed to link themes together. The questions posed and the themes addressed go beyond the bounds of a single subject as far as the qualities of water are concerned, and this requires a new planning strategy.

## Planning instruments and planning culture

Even since people have organized their surroundings, tilled fields, founded villages and settlements, they have had to make water into something they can use, and regulate water management. Thus water planning is one of the oldest driving forces in urban development, and gave rise to important engineering constructions at a very early stage in history. But these were always an expression of an attitude as well, of philosophy, myth and religion, they were presented aesthetically. Today it is scarcely possible to understand any longer how closely the fields of art, architecture and engineering were linked until the late Middle Ages: they formed a unit. An outstanding example of this kind of interdisciplinary work with water is an artist like Leonardo da Vinci.

In the course of history these fields have developed, become more specialized and moved apart. A real interplay of planning disciplines is rarely found, if at all. Architects like using choice sites near water, but it is exceptional for them to address other water themes and they usually see water as a hostile force that damages their buildings. Engineers are inclined to find purely technical solutions to questions about water, and often seem to be following a marked urge to convince others and themselves that those solutions are indispensable. Artists seldom make reference to this element that determines life and the environment. They often use water decoratively, as part of their own self-presentation system.

But water problems in town and in the countryside, which are increasing the world over – problems like surface and groundwater pollution, floods, drought and climatic change require holistic strategies and planning. Causes can often be found in the fact that such problems are linked with our social values and customs. Isolated repairs are of limited use only, in terms of both space and time. We are becoming increasingly aware of the necessity to work sustainably and far-sightedly with water. In the future planners will be increasingly required to put water itself back in a consistent context. This is the only appropriate way for dealing with its qualities and diversity. And here are some ideas for a start on integrated planning:

Global and local: Water always creates a relationship between detail and the whole. Each individual drop contributes to the balance of the earth's climate. Water projects become valuable when they help this process and can show that the place is being addressed, and how it is connected with the world around it.

Social significance: Water always stands for exchange and openness as well. It reflects fairness or injustice between human beings. Planning is successful if the cultural and social needs of the individual users are met and societies are regulated communally, and are expressed correctly.

Citizen involvement and participation: The way the most important substance for life on earth is handled is determined in many democratic countries by the priorities set by citizens. Water projects should include citizens and later users in planning and decision-making to as large an extent as possible.

Commitment and participation: It is important to promote and stimulate people's own creativity, as water is full of imagination, and a water-playground is one of the most popular places there are, and not just for children. Planning should offer people a chance to exert their influence and to suggest and agree to open possibilities for play.

Demonstrating sustainable environmental technologies: This means that processes for purifying and treating water, for avoiding floods and other such things should not be concealed, but wherever possible be presented openly and creatively. Retaining and managing rainwater in a new residential area can be integrated into open spaces within the planning process and become part of the architecture.

Admitting multi-functionality: This can be seen everywhere in nature. Why must a rainwater retention facility be used for this purpose only? Skilful planning means that play and sunbathing areas can be built in for when the weather is dry, as they won't be used for those purposes when it is raining anyway.

Integrated planning will always combine several water themes where possible. There are many of these, and they often do not exclude other types of use. But this can only succeed when everyone involved in the planning process really does use interdisciplinary working practices. Tolerance alone is nothing like sufficient here. The specialist disciplines should overlap in every individual involved, and every individual in a team should be aware of at least some elements of the others' specialist fields.

To do justice to water we have to go into the waterworld ourselves, experiment with it and learn to think in an integrated and interdisciplinary way about its flow and flexibility.

# The water system in Berlin's Potsdamer Platz

Visible water cleansing through a planted biotope does not just stabilize the water quality, but also adds a strikingly dune-like note to the austere urban landscape.

No parapet or railing – stepping stones lead over the expanse of urban water.

Large underground cisterns store rainwater from the roofs and make it available for reuse and supply of the water features.

Question after question cropped up on the top of the red Infobox in the middle of Potsdamer Platz, and deep abysses opened up in front of it. Colourful hard hats moved as though on invisible strings, and so did the lorries, full or empty after they had tipped their loads out, divers poured the cellar foundations into the groundwater at night, coloured piping ran to and fro over streets and excavations, cranes raised and lowered everything that was needed inside and outside, up there or down here. Expectations of the completed Potsdamer Platz were immense, and the problems on what was once Europe's largest building site were highly complicated. Two demands: people were not just supposed to work here, they were supposed to spend their leisure time here as well. A vibrant urban construct was to be created, which is difficult in the shadow of towering company headquarters. And the intention of setting high ecological standards for the project had caught on as well. There were the following problems: very little space was available for leisure provision, and it was subject to all sorts of demands and wishes. What devices for planning open space, what themes can be used to do justice to a lot of people and the urban design at the same time, and finally to come close to meeting ecological aims?

Herbert Dreiseitl had already worked on Potsdamer Platz immediately after the Wall came down, with an Anglo-German planning team. The theme of water as a defining element in the open space had convinced both the Senate and the investors from the outset. First of all the design possibilities caught their imagination, and secondly they were fired by the chance of meeting the ecological challenges. The suggestion that rainwater should be used for flushing toilets and watering green areas was met with interest. The same was true of the idea of using the rainwater that collected in the underground tanks to feed a water

Even when frozen over in winter, the water provides an interesting context for the architecture.

Everything comes together here: active life, prestigious architecture and a filigree pattern of water features that contain in fact just collected rainwater.

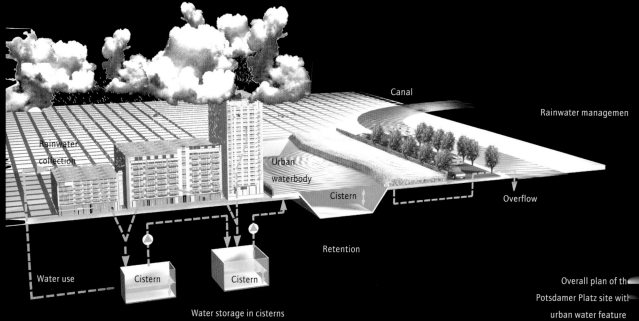

Rainwater collection

Canal

Rainwater managemen

Urban waterbody

Cistern

Overflow

Water use

Cistern

Cistern

Retention

Water storage in cisterns

Overall plan of th
Potsdamer Platz site witl
urban water feature

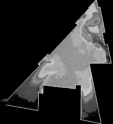

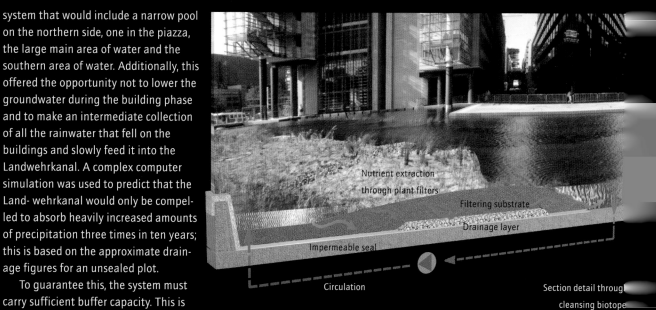

Nutrient extraction through plant filters

Filtering substrate

Drainage layer

Impermeable seal

Circulation

Section detail throug
cleansing biotope

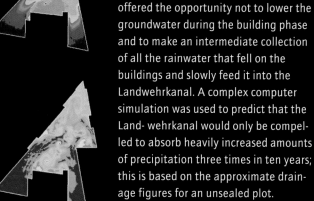

system that would include a narrow pool on the northern side, one in the piazza, the large main area of water and the southern area of water. Additionally, this offered the opportunity not to lower the groundwater during the building phase and to make an intermediate collection of all the rainwater that fell on the buildings and slowly feed it into the Landwehrkanal. A complex computer simulation was used to predict that the Land- wehrkanal would only be compelled to absorb heavily increased amounts of precipitation three times in ten years; this is based on the approximate drainage figures for an unsealed plot.

To guarantee this, the system must carry sufficient buffer capacity. This is provided in the first place by five underground tanks with a total volume of 2,600 cubic metres, of which 900 cubic metres are left free in their turn for cases of heavy precipitation. In addition to this, the main area of water can still offer a reserve of 15 centimetres between the normal and the maximum water level, which provides a storage buffer of 1,300 cubic metres. A key feature was the water resources that were discovered above the turbidity level of the main area of water. Solids can start to settle in the underground tanks before the water flows out of source vessels on the banks of the south and main areas of water, through planted purifi-

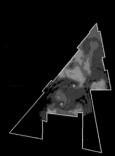

low simulation analysing
ow the water acts within
he geometry of the pool.
his made it possible to
ptimise the most effect
ocations for the inlet and
utlet points.

Sony Center

Potsdamer Platz

Philharmonie

A1

A2

A4

Weinhaus Huth

A3

Büro B4

Nordgewässer

Hyatt-Hotel A5

Piazza

Büro B5

Büro B6

D1
Spielbank

IMAX B7

Wohnen B8

D2
Theater

Staatsbibliothek

Wohnen B9

Debis
Hauptverwaltung

Volksbank C2

Hauptgewässer

Canarishaus

Südgewässer

C3

Landwehrkanal

Scharoun's Berlin
Philharmonie is reflected
in the crystal clear water.

Steps and sculpture
platform in the mobile
surface of the water.

Architecture bathed in
light, reflected and dissolved
in the water.

Turbulent rhythmic
structures.

The water surface is
a mirror at night.

Stippled waves, created by
the tiniest possible change
in levels, alternate with
smooth and turbulent areas.
The interplay of wind,
nature and art produces
visual colour games.

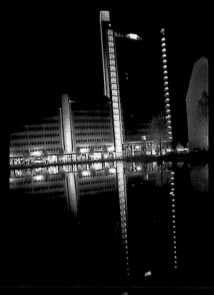

cation biotopes, where it is cleaned biologically and chemically. If necessary, technical filters can also be used, which will remove any floating algae in the summer months.

In Marlene-Dietrich-Platz water flows in intricate patterns to the lowest point in the piazza. The water glides of flowsteps from the main expanse of water, and here rhythmic wave structures are formed. A detail that is accurate to a millimetre, worked out in 1:1 models. Then, immediately adjacent to the piazza, the water drifts from two sides over linear wave cascades, creating a clear link with the architecture. Finally water also emerges from a source in the northern area of water, then flows down a narrow channel. Given the extremely complex criteria that had to be met, DaimlerChrysler representative Karl-heinz Bohn rightly pointed out after the opening that »as well as the fascination that this idea exercised over all of us, it soon became clear that an artificial expanse of water creates a number of problems if energy-intensive technology and chemical additives are not used.« The results are convincing, as the quality of the water is good, the buffer capacity is adequate and the use of fresh water in the buildings has been reduced. In design terms, the »Urban Water Feature« has given Potsdamer Platz a unique open space.

# The climate in the Nuremberg Prisma

The whole roof area of the complex feeds directly into a water cistern.

The glass building creates a pleasant atmosphere within the city centre. Waterwalls and luxuriant vegetation create a healthy atmosphere full of natural light.

When architect Frank Lloyd Wright built the famous »Fallingwater« house in the hilly countryside of Pennsylvania he had one thing above all in mind: he wanted to blend the building into the landscape of woodland, river and rock. He produced a masterpiece that overwhelms visitors mainly because of the way the torrent rushing under the building is handled. Here water does not just help to balance the climate in the house. You can see it in brick-lined pools, on smooth rocks when it rages into the basins in the natural stone. And you can hear it when the shell of the building changes acts as a resonating chamber to change the constant rushing into the natural music of a region.

A lot is possible out there in the forests of America that could not be done within the confines of a city; at best it has to undergo a transformation to work there. But the architectural aim of blending the inside and the outside

Lush vegetation compliments Joachim Eble's sustainable architecture.

51

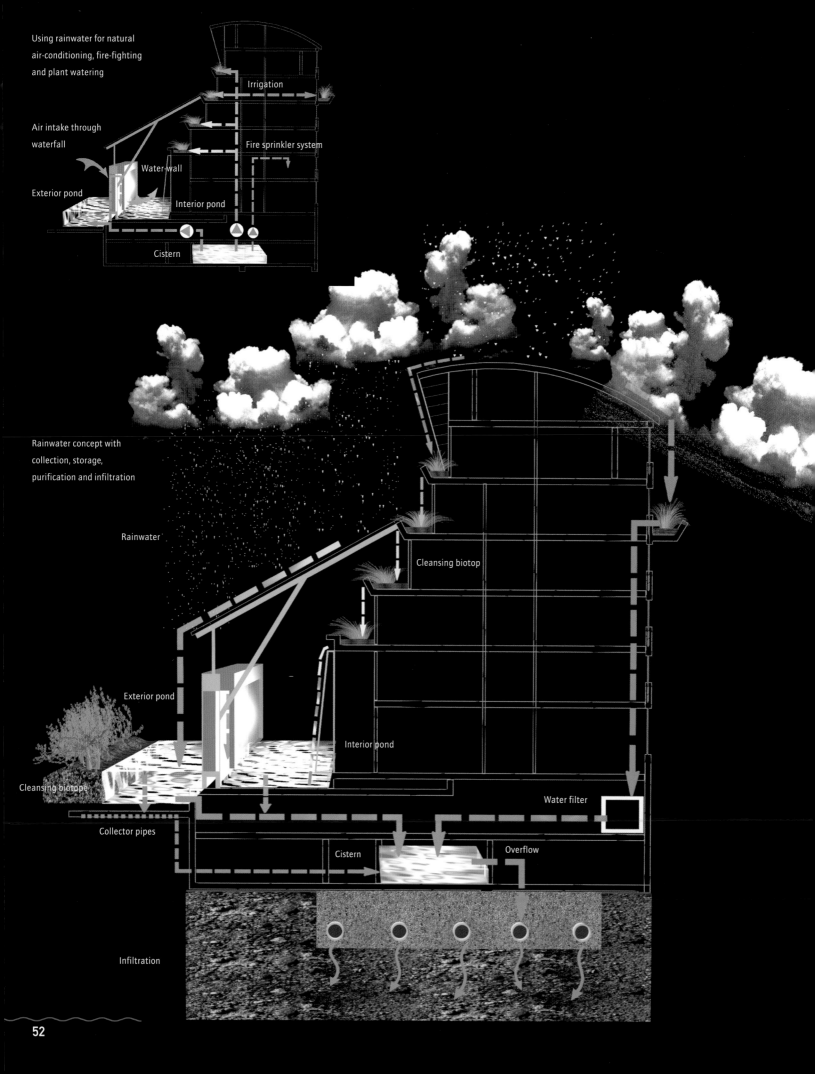

Using rainwater for natural
air-conditioning, fire-fighting
and plant watering

Irrigation

Air intake through
waterfall

Fire sprinkler system

Water-wall

Exterior pond

Interior pond

Cistern

Rainwater concept with
collection, storage,
purification and infiltration

Rainwater

Cleansing biotop

Exterior pond

Interior pond

Cleansing biotope

Water filter

Collector pipes

Cistern

Overflow

Infiltration

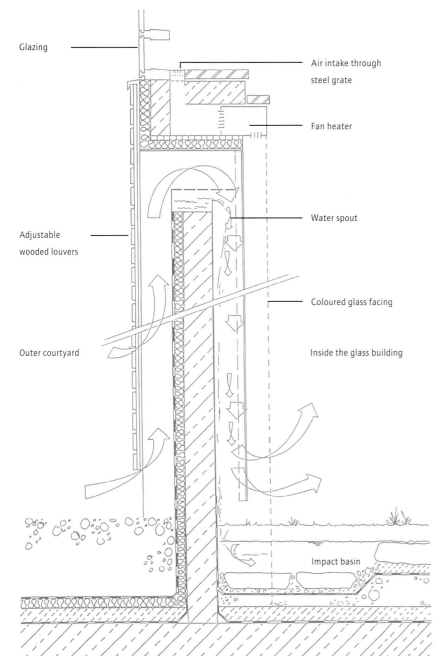

Glazing

Air intake through
steel grate

Fan heater

Water spout

Adjustable
wooded louvers

Coloured glass facing

Outer courtyard

Inside the glass building

Impact basin

applies in both places. In Nuremberg, for example, five waterfalls pout down at the same time into a set of residential and commercial premises that have been designed with a great deal of variety, using an entirely new design approach. In the »Prisma« – »Prism« – as the complex is called, removing boundaries was the key issue. Rainwater is of crucial importance here. All the water that falls on to the roofs flows through various cleaning phases into a tank with a capacity of just under 300 cubic metres, and is pumped from there into two circulating systems. Surplus water seeps into the ground under the underground car park. The first circulating system is used to supply the plants in the greenhouse, which extends over four storeys. South American vegetation grows in one section, Australian in the other, and both in a landscape of watercourses and ponds. These conservatories face south and south-west, and are part of the passive solar energy use concept.

High temperatures in the summer at least created a need for a second circulating system. Here the pump dispatches water to six water-walls, which has a number of positive effects. Even if you have never visited Fallingwater you know how the sound affects you. You breathe more deeply than you have for a long time, each individual alveolus seems to come to life. The effect of the water-walls is like that of waterfalls because the hydro-physical processes are the same: the water pulls air down with it, creating a light wind. In Nuremberg, water falls between two walls each five metres high, which forces air out at the bottom. This stream of water pulls in air through a slit in the wall, cleans it and cools it – at least in summer. In winter the water, which is at a minimum of 18 degrees, warms up the cool outside air. This positive effect on air temperature and humidity is associated with a visual one. This air-conditioning system, based on readily understandable prem-

Exterior vents supply the waterwalls with fresh air which is drawn down by the falling water, like in a natural waterfall, which is then filtered, moistened and blown out by the water into the interior at a wind speed of 3 m/sec. The system cools the building in the summer and heats it in the winter.

The greenhouse as a pleasant climate in the city centre. Water-walls and luxuriant vegetation create a healthy atmosphere and a flood of light.

53

The natural light flooded climatising waterwalls are artistically designed.

Making the glass sheets: The colour design is achieved by layering fragments of coloured glass.

Layering glass fragments produces a three-dimensional effect after fusing, and creates interesting effects of light and shade.

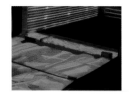

The natural light flooded climatising waterwalls are artistically designed

ises, is presented as an art object. The walls are suspended without frames, and glow in fascinating colours, particularly at night. At the same time the structure of the coloured layers, which were fused together at 760 degrees, is constantly changed by the water as it flows down. The water successfully pulls the sophisticated and varied design of the space together – with a contained dynamic and by providing background sound.

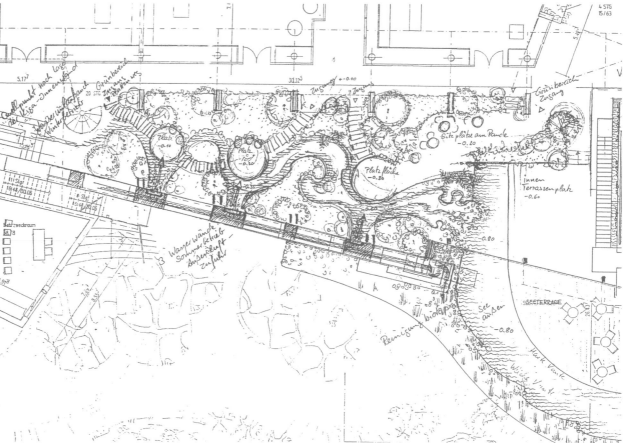

# Wind- and water-wheel in Owingen

The fact that rain is necessary but can be abominable often makes people feel that it never comes at precisely the right time. We feel similarly about wind, unless we are wanting to go sailing or fly a kite. Children usually see this differently. Wind and weather mean change to them. A lot of things emerge or start to move that weren't there before, or were standing still.

Herbert Dreiseitl wanted to make something positive of wet and stormy weather with his rainwater-wind device in Owingen, a small town in the hinterland of Lake Constance. The artwork has been at the extended primary and secondary school since the year 2000. As so often in his work, this object is based not just artistic, but also functional and even ecological. For technical or even financial reasons a decentralized, open rainwater concept was chosen, in which the lesser part of the water seeps away in a part of the building that is an attractive area in its own right.

The greater part seeps away outside in a system of hollows and trenches. But before the water turns the playing-field into a temporary pond, it sets a wind- and water-wheel installation in motion. Two wheels, each with two rotor blades and a water-wheel with six blue scoops turn when they are affected by wind or water from a roof area of 360 square metres. The three wheels are mounted on an axle with free bearings which in its turn is supported on an undulating concrete wall. At the highest point of the wall is a metal gutter that catches water from the roof and takes it to the scoops on the water-wheel from there its flows along an open gutter in the wall into a trench that in its turn takes the water under a path to the infiltration swale. But this undulating wall can only be a plaything to a certain extent. To protect the children from mechanical injuries from the wheels, a sheet of blue metal keeps the urge to climb within limits.

Water from the roof flows through a channel to a wind- and water-wheel, where it sets the wheels in motion.

The undulating wall with a rainwater channel is also suitable for play.

General plan of the drainage project for the new school wing. The majority of the water from the roof seeps into waiting layers of moraine gravel. Seepage pipes and basin and a trench under the building are used to retain the rainwater.

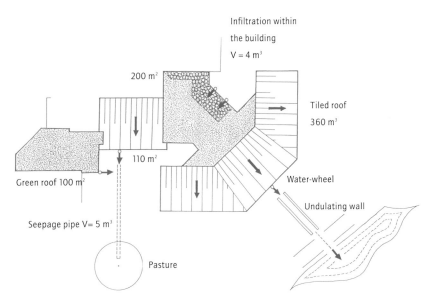

Infiltration within the building
V = 4 m³

200 m²

Green roof 100 m²

110 m²

Seepage pipe V= 5 m³

Pasture

Tiled roof
360 m³

Water-wheel

Undulating wall

Infiltration swale

Valuable rainwater is fed directly into the natural cycle via the wall into the wind and water artwork, via a wall gutter and infiltration swale into highly permeable layers of moraine gravel.

# Solar City Linz

The low-lying woodland has no strictly fixed boundaries, but access is provided via specific walkways, so that it is more or less impossible to wander randomly.

A lot of people would like to live and work in the same place, and this is also an accepted credo in urban development policy. It should be possible to realize life-plans for the population according to taste, in a graded system of upper, middle and lower centres in which both are possible without a great distance between them. But the queues of cars outside large towns every morning show the mess that trying to meet these wishes on a regional basis has got us into.

This time-consuming and air-polluting scene is played out in the Upper Austrian town of Linz every day as well. For this reason the city of 200,000 inhabitants and a proud 180,000 jobs looked for somewhere to build new housing estates. But it was difficult to find suitable building land, as Linz is confined between the Danube and the Traun. So a number of dreams are inevitably drowned, at least in the protected sphere of influence. But there is one dream that is due to come to fruition in 2003, very near these two rivers and what remains of a typical landscape of water meadows. Architects of the calibre of Richard Rogers, Norman Foster and Thomas Herzog were persuaded to work for this project, which was Austria's largest urban development scheme at the time. The Dreiseitl studio won the competition for designing the landscape architecture.

General view of the area during modelling and earthworks at the bathing lake. In the background is the Danube, and the large belt of woodland water meadows that is still in existence.

General plan of the new town with the new bathing lake, existing low-lying woodland and the green belt as a transitional area.

Spacious landscapes with individual, carefully placed points for resting or activities are the key design features of the town.

58

Woodland

Swimming lake

Solar Park

Creativity room

Landscape park

Town centre

Schools

Aumühl Creek

59

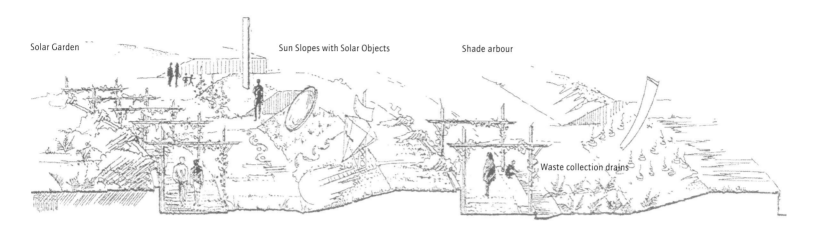

Solar Garden       Sun Slopes with Solar Objects       Shade arbour

Waste collection drains

Fine areas of wooded water meadows including the large and small Weikerl lakes are essential elements that have to be considered as part of the open-air concept for the new district.

The project was given the fine-sounding title Solar City Linz, and has raised enormous expectations. In the long term it is intended to provide a total of 25,000 people with homes in five centres. So far the concrete plans include one centre with about 32.5 hectares of building space for about 4,500 people, including about twenty hectares of open space. Doubts in terms of nature conservation are understandable. For this reason Linz's director of building, Franz Xaver Goldner, has assurances about demands and intentions: »The adjacent Traun-Danube water meadows will become a nature conservation area. Visitor control in the form of landscape-designed experience paths is intended to absorb the anticipated pressure from the population.«

This sets the open-space planners a difficult task. They have to fend off threats to the nature conservation area – and they have to do this without banning access, but by controlling it. The first thing to be controlled is rainwater, using a cleverly devised system of channels, basins, ponds and streams, extending from the area near the buildings to the wooded meadows. Groundwater upgrading, the creation of permanent and temporary wet areas and supporting the water regime in the river meadows are at the top of the priority list.

To protect the existing meadows from excessive visitor numbers, a range of different recreation areas will be established between Solar City and the

nature conservation area: playgrounds, tenants' gardens and meeting places are in the immediate vicinity of the housing estate. Next to this is a park-like green corridor with room for a broad range of uses and then come the usual recreational facilities available near a city: a bathing lake, existing allotments and a new sports centre. Then all the people who want to move on to the meadows will be funnelled into walkways, given information at specially established stations and guided to specific places. Solar City will only be accepted and successful if the ambitious open-air project is implemented logically and consistently. Then it could possibly become a pilot project.

In the green areas between the new town and the bathing lake mounds and hills are created using left-over soil from the construction site.

Woodland

Nature trail

Swimming lake

Lake kiosk

Solar garden

Creativity room

Festival plaza

# Rainwater for the bears in Zurich zoo

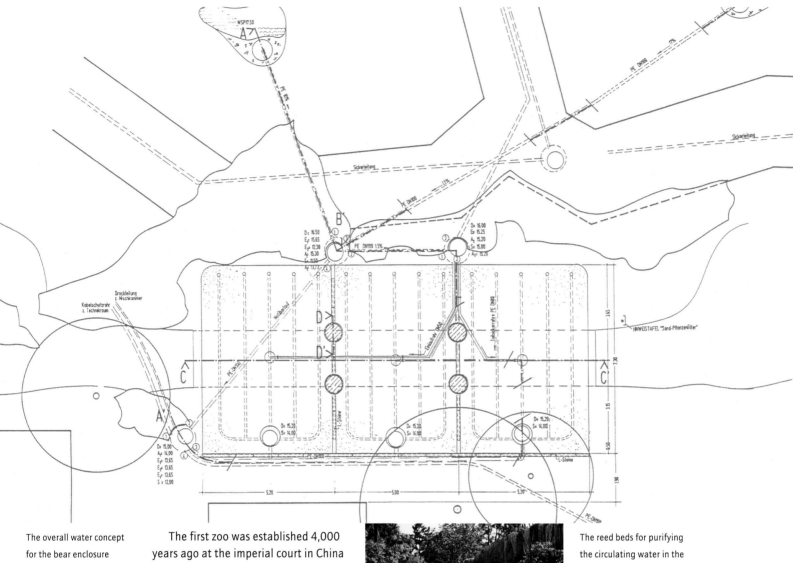

The overall water concept for the bear enclosure showing the position of the purification beds, pipes, shafts and drainage ducts.

Even though they are a long way from home – at least the water and the rest of their immediate surroundings should be right for the bears in Zurich zoo.

The first zoo was established 4,000 years ago at the imperial court in China with a few exotic animals, followed 2,300 years ago by Alexandria and 420 years ago by Augsburg. Until the modern period, interesting mammals, above all bears, roamed in ramparts and fortification ditches, contained in special pits or enclosures. Zoos have been with us for some time as institutions – though its functions have changed. In the age of extinction the show-places of yesterday are changing into reserves for animals that are under threat. The WWF's koala bear identifies an enclosure as the last resort on every second information board. But the view through the fence is far from revealing the gratitude of gibbon, gnu or giraffe. And the visitor's expression is often similar to that of the sad koala bear, who can find little that is pleasurable in the change from a danger-filled existence to a life with full board and medical care.

Zoos have to change again, and offer more room to fewer animals. The zoo in

The reed beds for purifying the circulating water in the bear enclosure fit in with the overall image.

The water is purified in the reed beds, which are bound into the overall design by a walkway.

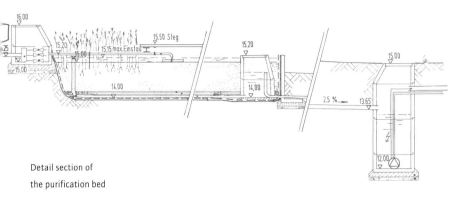

Detail section of
the purification bed

Even the fish feel at home in
the ponds, which shows how
good the water quality is.

Zurich, Switzerland, plays a leading part
in this field on the world stage. Working
on a master plan dating from 1993, this
zoo wants to go over to keeping animals
in way that is appropriate to the species,
so that their basic needs in terms of
landscape can be considered. And this
twenty-year programme also tries to
make a contribution to conserving
resources: the Zurich animals' basic
water needs in their habitat will be met

with recycled rainwater. The Zurich planner Walter Vetsch is responsible for new
landscape design and modifications, but
Herbert Dreiseitl's studio has taken on
the water technology. The bear enclosure was the first part of the project to
be completed, in 1995, followed by the
waterfowl area in summer 1997, and
the sea-lion and ape areas are at the
planning stage.

It is not just animals that live in
water all the time, like sea-lions, for
instance, that make heavy demands on
water resources, bears too need clean
water. This need is met by collecting
rainwater from the surrounding paths
and green areas and storing it in underground tanks. These feed the circulating
system in the bear enclosure. The water
is pumped up to a rocky plateau, then
runs down an impressive waterfall six
metres high and three metres wide
into the bear enclosure, then flows in
a stream to two little lakes. It is a considerable challenge to use a compara-
tively simple technique to process surface and circulating water in a way that
is aesthetically appealing and drinkable
for the animals. Part of the cycle of
2,000 litres per minute trickles alter-
nately through one of a total of three
filter beds in a vertical direction, before
being returned to the water cycle.

A skilfully camouflaged gap in the
ground prevents the bears from getting
to the filter beds, though visitors are
allowed to do so. They can cross the
pools on a wooden walkway and convince themselves that great efforts are
being made to manage water in a way
that is ecologically sound. The zoo in
Zurich has found an impressive way
towards a new zoo strategy – and others
will follow.

These waterfalls are part
of the water cycle, and the
purification beds reduce the
proportion of fresh water
needed dramatically.

Slide valves, controls,
distributors

# Sonnenhausen estate in Glonn

The magnificent historical Sonnenhausen estate was given a water garden for rainwater management and to purify waste water. It is part of the little park.

There are all sorts of stories and legends about Karl Ludwig Schweisfurth. By profession a business management graduate and master butcher, he took over his father's sausage business in Herten, built it up into a company with 5,000 employees and sold it to a food concern in 1985. He used the profit to set up the Schweisfurth Foundation, and since then he has run an estate in Glonn, about 40 kilometres south of Munich, where he has realized his dream of alternative agriculture. Schweisfurth always had an affinity with art – he used to share this with his colleagues, and now he shares it with his animals. This story is told about the Hermannsdorfer Landwerkstätten, which are part of his property: he once painted the I-ging sign on the wall of a cowshed, which apparently by chance enticed two cows out of a corner of the shed. They put their heads on one side, then raced out into the fields to fetch their grazing friends. All the cows looked at the painting together until one of their number licked it off.

Rainwater is collected from the roofs of the building and fed into the water cycle via sweeping channels and fords.

Land art objects as viewpoints above the water garden.

Schweisfurth later had some more durable works of art set up on the site, plain stone columns for the Landwerkstätten, and striking wheels made of willow for the Sonnenhausen estate. The Sonnenhausen estate is next door to the Landwerkstätten, and has established itself as the seminar building for environmental education. The outdoor facilities were redesigned in 1989, largely on the basis of plans by the Dreiseitl studio.

Water running round a fireplace – elemental contrasts in the closest possible proximity.

In accordance with the aims of the foundation, all waste water is taken to planted purification tanks near the adjacent wood, then on to a stream after it has been cleaned. A large proportion of the rainwater flows into various ponds that determine the aesthetic of the open spaces and are also used to water the vegetables and flowers that are grown. When it rains, the water accumulates in the yard in paved channels leading to the pumped water cycle, which

Pulsating water movements appear in the flowforms, aerating and activating the water that flows through them.

feeds a well dating from the twenties. A curved channel runs out of the yard of the living section, swings to the right through flowform pools, circles a paved fireplace and finally ends up in a semi-natural pond.

Thus seminar themes on sustainable methods can be tested outside the conference rooms against the example of water management.

# Bathing-pond near Salzburg

Water cleaned by an aerating cascade (flowforms)

Sustainable water purification by natural symbiosis on the edge of the pond

The entire feature, with the wooden platform for the flowform cascade and purification biotope

»But rarity also insists upon a responsibility that makes the relationship more intimate – and the richness more valuable still.« This is the sort of thing that could be found in a glossy brochure for a rare and valuable product. Many species of plant and animal have become rarities – and that is why the above sentence in fact appears in a book about private swimming ponds, explaining the authors' motivation for creating these ponds. They want to provide a habitat for plants that have become rare and to give users a chance to observe things from a walkway or a bank with wild vegetation that show natural contexts and answer questions from experience even before they are asked.

Long before swimming pond euphoria set in, Herbert Dreiseitl installed a pond in a private garden near Salzburg that carried nature conservation ideas into the private sphere and in fact into a part of it where the opposite effect was usually made by a walled, sterile swimming bath. Five years later he extended the facility to 800 square metres, of which the surface of the water alone accounts for 400 square metres.

Excellent water quality is a key feature of a swimming pond. This is ensured here by two circulation systems. The first one pumps water from the 180 centimetre deep bathing area to the edge and into a densely planted marsh bed where it is purified. From there it flows through a filtration passage. As in the purification area, plant substrate is present on the membrane to a thickness of 50 centimetres, though in this case it is not immersed in water. From here it returns to the bathing area, purified.

Another circulation system pumps water to a higher point above the wooden platform, from which it cascades through flowform basins into the swimming pool. This enriches the water with oxygen and thus aerates the whole mass of water. As well as this, the water flowing through the flowforms creates a

pleasantly discreet but entirely perceptible pulsating sound background.

Bathing ponds are booming – perhaps because people can use them to turn a luxurious experience into a contribution to nature conservation.

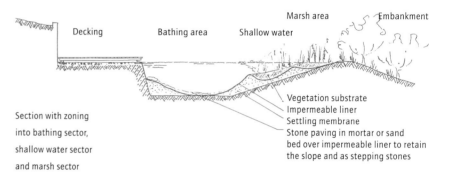

Section with zoning into bathing sector, shallow water sector and marsh sector

Decking · Bathing area · Shallow water · Marsh area · Embankment

Vegetation substrate
Impermeable liner
Settling membrane
Stone paving in mortar or sand bed over impermeable liner to retain the slope and as stepping stones

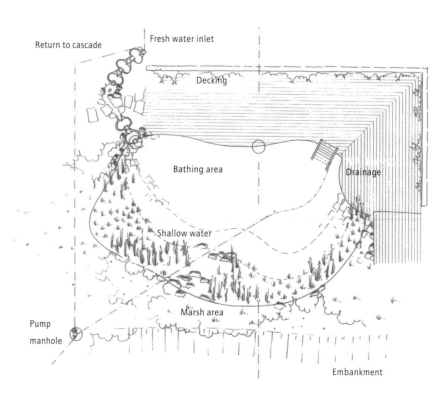

Return to cascade · Fresh water inlet · Decking · Bathing area · Drainage · Shallow water · Marsh area · Pump manhole · Embankment

# Rainwater management in Coffee Creek, Indiana, USA

Without their craving for new things, without their inventiveness we would probably still not drink Coca-Cola, not put on baseball caps, would still pay cash at the petrol station and write our books and articles on typewriters. Americans enjoy their extravagant lifestyle, but inevitably come up against barriers from time to time, and are thus constantly looking for ways round them.

For example, the United States has come perilously close to an abyss with its settlement policy. There seems to be no lack of land, and yet it is worth nothing without the resource of water, and this is now scarce in a number of places. And so a project developer in the state of Indiana is laying the foundation stone for a model settlement that can also set standards. It is strongly oriented towards pedestrians and cyclists, efficient energy use, healthy building materials and development density, and as well as all this it is highly committed to intelligent water management. The only water worth mentioning before building started is Coffee Creek, from which the area takes its name.

In 1996, Herbert Dreiseitl made contact with an American planning group, and three years later he joined the team of landscape architects and hydraulic engineers responsible for sections of the creative and hydraulic open air planning for Coffee Creek. The project makes additional heavy demands because it is close to a conservation area. A master plan fixed the main rainwater management requirements: precipitation water flows via trenches with slits to infiltration areas that are topographically staggered one behind the other. These are completely planted with prairie vegetation with roots systems that are highly water absorbent. The entire system would be able to contain once-in-a-century crisis rainfall within the area and allow it to soak away.

Detention swale with
local prairie vegetation

Trenches channel the
water from streets
and parking areas.

Pedestrian bridge
under construction

An estate intended to provide 1,200 residential units can only be built in an ecologically acceptable way with a cleverly devised system for the water technology infrastructure. But this infrastructure will not be visible – in fact the water will appear in natural stream beds, in ponds that run into each other over massive cascades piled up from natural stone slabs, producing a charming open space.

This complex water management will enable typical woods and prairies areas to survive – also because the entire water situation of the area, which covers a total of 260 hectares, will remain unchanged.

Soakaway trenches
for rainwater

The new settlement at
Coffee Creek was given a
central park. Sustainable
rainwater management
was developed for the area
as a whole.

# Think global, act local

Wolfgang F. Geiger

**Water is neither inexhaustible nor invulnerable. But the intensity with which it is used today tends to ignore these facts, as we increasingly exploit and pollute this gift of nature that is so essential for life. If we do not want to have to dig for our own water in future, we must think co-operatively, decentralize, and establish autonomous systems for water use at a local level.**

There is no other natural resource on which mankind makes such heavy and complex demands as it does on water. Although it is not renewable in part, we neglect it far more than other resources – just remember how oil exploitation was co-ordinated internationally. In contrast with this, we treat water as though it were inexhaustible. Philosophy, science and technology have contributed to this mistaken assessment.

On the whole, people prefer and have always preferred to establish towns near water. It can then be exploited directly, it is a transport medium that promotes trade, and it contributes to the well-being of the inhabitants. Water in a town fulfils cultural, architectural and social functions. The urban hydrologist Murray McPherson was emphatically pushing for planning of the water economy to meet social and ecological requirements as early as 1970.

Water was comprehensively studied and managed even in ancient cites like Miletus. This requires creativity that can combine art and design, social perceptions, insights into handling water and technical innovation. It was probably this universal appeal that inspired so many scholars to occupy themselves with water. Thales of Miletus (624 to 545 BC) reflected on the water cycle, Plato (427 to 347 BC) later philosophized about it and Palissy (1510 to 1590) provided scientific justifications. Annually recurring precipitation or springs and rivers that never dry up give people the feeling that water is limit-lessly available – which is often reflected today in senseless use of water in precisely those cities where there is a drought. In recent times, despite all the insights and knowledge about it, water has become a utility whose origins we do not think about, that we simply use and throw away.

Towns have always been the heaviest water users. If local supplies were not sufficient, water was brought from near and far – according to the technology available. Thus the resource was exploited beyond the extent to which it could be renewed, and the natural water cycle was permanently damaged. The devastating effects of urban growth and user behaviour were simply not seen at first. Increasingly more efficient technologies opened up new supplies like deep groundwater, for example, that could not be regenerated. Large dams on rivers in arid areas, often the life-arteries for many different peoples, may show the life-giving attributes of water, but they can also be a threat to peace. Low water charges, well below its market value, have also led to errors of judgement about the availability of water. Thus users remain unaware of the price they are really paying for water, and this leads to careless handling of the resource. For example, in an Indian community in which there was a major drought, water was brought in at great expense and distributed free of charge. This meant that users were not able to recognize the true value of water and left the taps running night and day even when no water was being used. This was justified by pointing out that the water did not cost anything.

There has been a failure to take precautions when dealing with water in the past. Problems arising from excessive consumption were often not recognized in time. And then when the problems were recognized they did not all generate appropriate pressure leading to political action, not all the solutions that were determined politically led to decisions that could be implemented, and those decisions did not all lead to concrete measures. Such measures were frequently consequence-driven, local case-by-case decisions that were made in response to damage, but not to causes. Here the »enemy approach« was generally taken: excess or dirty water had to be removed from towns as quickly as possible. Measures were designed to meet a purpose, and not integrated into comprehensive planning appropriate to the complexity of the water cycle. Thus the groundwater level was inevitably lowered in many urban areas, flooding increased, and natural plant and animal habitats were destroyed.

The larger cities become, the more they seem to use water regardless of the consequences. For example, Peking is a city with millions of inhabitants. The groundwater level is going down annually by over two metres, but water is used for air conditioning plants, cleaning cars and street cleaning, huge sprinkler systems are installed for green areas and rainwater is removed from the city in large channels. A Mediterranean tourist uses a thousand litres of water a day, even though it is a particular scarce commodity in the region in the summer months. Water is wasted all over the world, in countries with rapidly growing cities that are in the early stages of industrialization, in industrialized countries growing at a moderate rate, in regions that have little water and regions that have a lot of water. At the same time there are already a billion people who do not have adequate supplies of drinking water, two billion people have no sanitary facilities and four billion people produce contaminated water that is not subsequently purified to a sufficient extent. Additionally, thoughtless introduction of harmful chemicals and bacteriologically polluted sewage into the ground and water often makes the water unusable unless it is expensively purified. Far too little attention is paid to the hidden chemical time bombs that are lying in wait in the ground and in sediments. These harmful materials could be reactivated by changed land use or climatic changes.

Thus present-day development of cities is often at the expense of future generations, and the gravest errors of urban history are repeated: the environment is massively damaged to achieve short-term economic advantage and growth, and the profit drawn from this helps to make good the grossest of the environmental damage. Many developing countries are starting to make the same ecological mistakes as the industrialized countries. Cities often grow in developing countries before a solid economic basis exists, and above all before the necessary infrastructure is in place. There are few cities with the resources and personnel to provide their rapidly growing population with clean water and sanitation. As the majority of people will be living in cities for the first time in a few years time (an estimated 60% by 2025; the urban population will double between 2000 and 2025 in South America, Africa and South-East Asia), the water problem will become more acute.

Mega-cities like the one in the Pearl River Delta between Hong Kong and Guangzhou or Japan's Tokaido Corridor between Tokyo, Nagasaki and Asaka are considered to be a rela-tively new phenomenon: a number of individual cities have grown together to form regional urban landscapes. Traditional water supply and disposal techniques no longer work because of their sheer size.

All attempts to secure a social and ecological balance on the basis of traditional environment protection measures only increase the imbalance. This means that even greater problems will have to be faced in the future. Changing patterns of employment and social structure can rapidly lead to the decline of cities, to unemployment with all its social consequences and to an inability to cope with toxic industrial waste that has been improperly disposed of.

Even the responsible politicians are gradually realizing that economic development and the condition of the environment, including water availability, can no longer be treated separately. Irresponsible use of water as a resource limits growth and rapidly destroys what has been created. Thus poverty is at the same time both a principal cause and a principal effect of urban water problems.

As globalization proceeds, even today cities are caught up in world-wide economic competition. If sustainable economic development is to be secured, some rethinking is necessary: water requirements must be made dependent on the water that is available on the spot and in the immediate vicinity – water must not be brought in regardless of the environment

and expense. A distinction has to be made between the elemental basic requirement, an additional social requirement and an economic requirement. We should remember the Roman system of water distribution, as it has survived in Nîmes. Here the supplies to public wells, commercial operations, baths and private houses were staggered so that water was obtainable in each case only when supplies were adequate. If water was short, only the basic public requirement was covered.

Water management can only be balanced if social and economic wishes are covered by the quantities of available and renewable water. We have to accept that urban water concepts cannot be based on prefabricated models, whether they are local or imported. Water problems must be solved specifically and within the immediate vicinity for every town, every district and even every neighbourhood. Something that works for a town can be inappropriate in a particular neighbourhood. Realizing this compels us to decentralize responsibility and action. There are many reasons for this. Large supply and disposal systems cost far more than small, autonomous systems. Small units are far less prone to faults. They bring small and middle-sized enterprises together to construct and maintain them, and thus reinforce socio-economic structures. Small, autonomous systems remain able to function because the people running and using them identify with their system and see it as their property. »Water neighbourhoods« are also better able to take responsibility for preventive measures.

Decentralized water management fails only occasionally, but still does fail because of the structure of the water authorities. They are centrally organized and their responsibilities broken down independently: watering green areas, drinking water or sewage, for instance. As no distinction is made between different uses, this means high costs for water of uniform quality. As well as this, central systems are geared to peak requirements, because they have to cover end-user needs directly at every hour of the day and night. This too suggests a concept in which central water supplies meet a basic load and keep neighbourhood reservoirs full all the time, for example. This opens up new possibilities for reducing water losses, as narrower supply pipe widths can be used, meaning that cladding or smaller pipework can be introduced in existing supply systems.

So solving water problems in town requires a dual system. Technically speaking, local resources have to be used. Rainwater management is the key to the future. Water is part of a cycle in which it is used to water green areas and feed ponds that enhance the value of the immediate environment. Local people take the initiative in small-scale water-neighbourhoods. Public water supplies can then be reduced to covering a basic load, dependent on local climatic conditions. Economic responsibility is taken for a small area: the water neighbourhoods have to buy water in from central suppliers. In terms of water prices, a clear distinction has to be made between value, costs and tariffs. Here the real cost of supply and disposal has to be met by the user.

This system has a chance of success in the mega-cities because of the living conditions there: people live in a confined local environment, and spend their evenings and weekends in the immediate vicinity. They rely on local shopping facilities and leisure activities. Thus as a rule town-dwellers lead a life that is restricted to the locality, regardless of the size of their town. So the city of the future will have to be a city of neighbourhoods in which life-style and development are determined on a small scale. The central water authorities then follow the wholesale principle and sell to the neighbourhood units, who then manage their water internally.

The question remains of how long it will take to rethink in this way. Hesiod established the basic link between water pollution and the health of townspeople as early as 800 BC. At that time it took about three centuries for the Greek cities to introduce sanitary installation of the kind that already existed in the early cultures of Mesopotamia and on the Indus. We are faced with a learning process that will start in school and continue throughout our lifetimes. Whatever happens, this new way of dealing with water can only come from the inside, from the user.

Solving local problems by taking local measures does not exclude global action, especially as local water problems often have a lot in common. Hydrological and technical principles, the build-up of small water units and strategies for solutions that save expense and resources are transferable. Water-saving technologies can be used everywhere. Constantly rising demand, senseless use and mismanagement can be countered world-wide, by control through price. It is possible to lay down global requirements that all users are considered, river catchment areas are treated as hydrographic and economic units and that integrated overall water planning is set up to do this. The economic value of water is reflected in the price everywhere, and water users are involved in solving their problems, they can help to determine the course of events.

As eco-systems do not respect national boundaries, internationally agreed water management is essential. But within this global network the regulation systems must leave sufficient scope for regional and local implementation. It would be wrong to see globalization as doing everything in the same way. The basic principles must be recognized globally and implemented by regulation – then the appropriate solutions have to be found locally.

Global action should lead to solidarity in dealing with water. Here responsibility still lies with the industrialized countries. They are in a good position economically, and must therefore begin to implement the new thinking, particularly as they have dumped the cost of their growth on to nature and the environment in the past. Here making pretty declarations of intent about water protection is just as inadequate as suggesting to developing countries that they should handle their resources carefully. The development and environmental crises that the industrialized countries went through in the eighties have still not been fully overcome.

Global economic competition between cities must be transformed into global competition for the best ecological conditions, which will make cities economically competitive in the long term again.

It would be good in the year 2030 to be able to look back and say: in the last quarter of the 20th century pilot projects were started that created locally independent water concepts that secured people's basic water needs and also used local water resources following nature's model. And they also helped to maintain valuable eco-systems, at the same time offering people an environment that was worth living in, thus becoming a model for all new building and redevelopment models for the first decade of the 21st century. In many places, renewal went hand in hand with a change of thinking that no longer saw water as an everyday item to be used and then thrown away. Everyone recognised the true value of water. Globalization of markets and the media meant that these ideas spread quickly. The water problems that the 20th century had left behind were visibly alleviated.

In the second decade of the 21st century water neighbourhoods emerged in all towns and cities, and they took joint responsibility for designing and maintaining their immediate surroundings. Every household was geared towards economical and careful use of water. Municipal and regional privately funded institutions, linked with river catchment areas, were responsible for supplying the local water neighbourhoods and dealt with surplus water, preparing it for repeated use. A trade network was established between neighbourhoods, towns and the surrounding agricultural areas. Responsibility for water administration was completely separated from the supply and disposal infrastructure, which was geared to economic viability.

In the third decade of the 21st century, which has just ended, trade with water came to be taken for granted, with the price related to the true value of the water. State authorities retained only regulatory and controlling functions, and agreed these internationally and globally. The global network of main suppliers and locally based water neighbourhoods worked increasingly well. The neighbourhoods met emergencies within a restricted area to as large an extent as possible or increased the amount of water they drew from suppliers outside the region. Local people took full responsibility for their immediate area, and made this more worth-while to live in. New life was breathed into the water-related cultural heritage. Nature started to play a major part in the megacities again as a lung and open space, and as a shell for emotional and physical existence. The dual system had proved its worth and led to sustainable development appropriate to the needs of the present generation and not limiting the possibilities available to future generations.

This state of affairs was achieved as a result of perceptions and farsightedness at the turn of the 20th and 21st centuries. Thus today the whole world has become an urban network that is capable of acting rapidly on a local basis, and thus of surviving.

# Rainwater retention on the Kronsberg in Hanover

We heard a great deal about the Kronsberg – before and after Expo 2000. But when the bulldozers have finally moved away, perhaps it will only be the local residents who find their way up this 43 metre hill. Which would be a pity. Whatever else happened, the Kronsberg development was one of the exhibits off the main World Fair site that was marketed and realized under the motto »Man – Nature – Technology« as a model ecological project. As is well known, this challenge was not met in all fields.

The »slope avenues« under construction; the stream is fitted with sheet seal.

One field in which it was successful, however, was the rainwater management in this new urban district of 130 hectares. The head of Hanover's environment department applied the word »revolutionary« to this approach, which promised that the hydrological conditions would not deteriorate despite the sealing which the development made inevitable. The idea was that not a drop of rainwater that fell on roofs, roads and squares would be taken into the sewerage system, but would be retained on the Kronsberg or at its foot, soak away in part and feed a valuable body of water underneath, even in dry periods. This was largely achieved by two green areas, 13 by 30 metres, running parallel with the slope and various bands of parkland arranged one behind the other along the bottom of the slope. These three strips received all the surface water from the districts that could not soak away, evaporate or be retained in the private and semi-private areas, and in the district parks.

Regulating devices are built into the retention lips. This means that the outflow can be varied and the retention frequency controlled.

The retention and soakaway areas on the slope and at its foot are rightly called open spaces. Compulsory ecological measures are not seen as technical facilities here, but as parks. Water, even when it is intended to flow away slowly, or disappear by infiltration, and thus not a permanent feature, is an exciting and enhancing sight for all age groups in the green areas. In the two »slope avenues«

At the foot of the slope the retention basins hold back rainwater to slowly release it over time.

on the southern and northern peripheries of the development the planners made use of the slope of approximately 5 % with a cascade design. A naturally extended stream bed runs through the two green areas and takes the water to one of nine terraced basins, where it is retained until it soaks away. If there is very heavy rainfall the surplus water flows over the concrete retention lips, drawn on the site as civilization lines, and down into the next basin. The stream produced in this way is piped under intersecting roads, and footpaths run through the bed of the stream on reinforced fords. The water is intended to remain visible for longer in some basins which are an additional 30 centimetres lower and reinforced with a cohesive substrate. These are mainly in the areas along the foot of the slope and take up the water from the two sloping avenues and the surface water from the base road running parallel with the long side. A wooden regulating device set in the retention lip makes it possible to control the outflow quantity individually.

The Kronsberg definitely deserves a place as a show project in terms of rainwater management for a settlement of this size. It is worth a visit – perhaps especially after the World Fair.

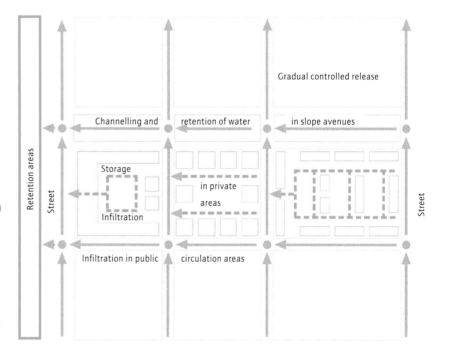

Retention areas | Street | Channelling and | retention of water | in slope avenues | Gradual controlled release | Street

Storage / Infiltration — in private areas

Infiltration in public — circulation areas

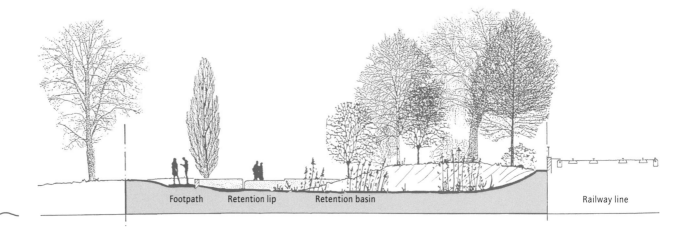

Section through retention areas at the foot of the slope

Footpath    Retention lip    Retention basin    Railway line

Development plan showing
areas built by the year 2000.
The sloping avenues and
retention areas show up
as linear strips of urban
parkland.

# The Scharnhauser Park in Ostfildern

The original barracks and
the topographical structure.

Topography and urban
structure of the area
as a whole

Part of the landscape
steps with the basin
cascades, plan and section

Barracks architecture traditionally has little in common with the quality of life. The buildings are arranged and developed from a purely functional point of view, and people are not intended to feel particularly at home. And at the time the people who commissioned them were scarcely concerned to address the ecological consequences of building. The Allied Forces have been leaving Germany and going home for years now. Quite frequently they leave run-down military accommodation behind, often extensive sites that had little money spent on them and that are usually more of an inherited problem than a welcome gift.

But these sites also have their own potential. They certainly take pressure off the town to provide new building land. But a new estate is only likely to succeed if the planners are creative and the barracks site meets modern requirements both inside and out. As in the case in the Scharnhauser Park near Ostfildern. This project involves 150 hectares, and is the largest urban development scheme in the Stuttgart area in the early 21st century. The 2002 regional horticultural show is at the heart of the site, and thus high on the list of regional priorities. Horticultural shows are increasingly inclined towards innovative approaches to town planning, and so it was clear from the beginning of the planning process that rainwater would have to be treated in a new way as well.

Two systems of streams flow below the site, which is on a south-facing slope, and the Scharnhauser Park surface water is useful to these. The Körsch, for example, often threatens to dry up in summer. Additional water would sustain the valuable biotope structure that is the only network worth speaking of in this region for sustaining flora and fauna. On the other hand, to avoid floods, the planners have settled for a different strategy of discharge reduc-

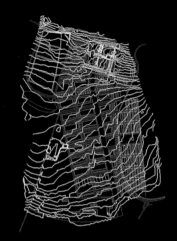

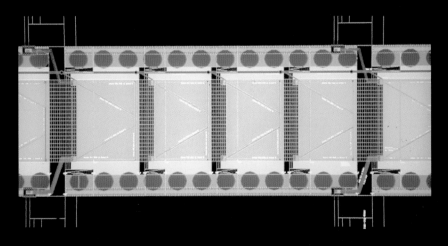

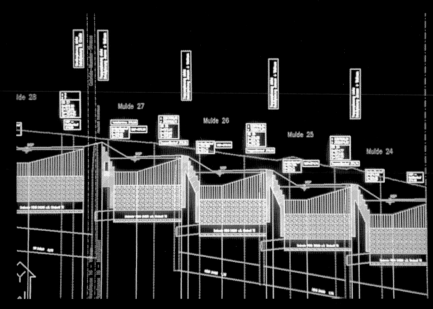

Site plan showing
rain water management

RKB West

RKB Ost

RKB Kreuzbrunnen

Höfelbach

Slope

Krähenbach

Retention areas

Filter-swale system

Rainwater channelling

81

tion, discharge delay and modest infiltration into the clayey subsoil.

The rainwater has now been fully withdrawn from the former mixed water sewer and now flows, when it has not been retained in private storage tanks or in roof gardens, or has soaked away through water-permeable surfaces, through a system of channels and ditches running alongside the streets. This network runs through the new estate as an unmistakable design feature. Here the cascade-like landscape steps, 1.5 kilometres long, are particularly striking. This design element is also part of the rainwater management programme: below the steps the living bottom zone purifies the water in additional retention hollows and pools. Discharged water that has been delayed and purified in this way is fed via natural gradients into the surrounding landscape, with its valuable wetlands, biotopes and spring areas.

Even if traces of the former military structure show in the urban development, the water has successfully linked up with the surrounding landscape and its features.

# Living in the Backum valley in Herten

Areas of water fed exclusively by rainwater put their stamp on the image of the estate, creating a high-quality waterscape.

Play areas and small paths are built into the green areas and link up with the drainage elements.

Small decentralized accumulation areas help to make the rainwater flow away more slowly.

Balance sheets were drawn up with great vigour at the end of the Emscher Park International Building Exhibition. Costs against profits, planned against actual visitor numbers, newly sealed against unsealed surfaces. But there was the occasional gloomy note sounded amid the general rejoicing about the considerable increase in public open and wooded spaces, and areas of water. Despite this increase the overall area that is not built up has been diminished over the past ten years. This has to do with a branch of industry, ailing for some time, a land user that has hardly been noticed by the Ruhr's land-use jugglers, that hardly fits in with the image of the area: agriculture.

One such area is to be found about a kilometre from the centre of the town of Herten on the northern edge of the Ruhr. This was the only IBA settlement project to use former agricultural land – though with intensive attention to landscape ecology during the planning process. And in addition to this, the town set itself the goal of creating affordable housing on the principles of ecological building, and thus living up to its slogan: Herten – technology and quality of life.

The promises have been kept. A thousand people will live on 13 hectares completely free of cars in the centre of the estate; generously and yet simply designed open spaces permit a wide variety of uses, public and private spaces blend together in the individually designed residential streets. Effective neighbourhood schemes establish the principles by which the use of open space is planned.

One of the landscape architects' principal tasks was optimizing water management. In just the same way as the general ecological programme, they wanted to make sure that water was managed in such a way that things were not worse than they had been before. This aim was achieved with a decentralized rainwater management concept.

Paved gutters are built into the residential streets sensitively, and carry the rainwater visibly to green areas near the estate.

Special attention has to be paid to the appropriate reinforcement when constructing the open swales.

Water from roofs and streets flows into open gutters then soaks away in grassed basins and open swales or accumulates in retention pools. The subsoil is cohesive, so only a small quantity of water soaks away from the basins and open swales, the effect derives more from delayed discharge and from raising the low water level of the Backum brook. Soiled water from the collective car parks at the edge of the estate are prepared for this running water by treatment with light density material precipitators and in purification biotopes. Residents are given an artistic reminder of the dominant theme behind the plans for their estate by a fountain and the watercourse that flows into it.

This new residential development is able to hold its own utterly and completely in terms of the former agricultural use because of the ecologically effective factors involved.

Rainwater from the roofs and streets slowly seeps away through the open swales into the green areas.

Hollows and open swales staggered in the form of cascades take the water from roofs, paths and squares for rainwater treatment in the semi-public green area.

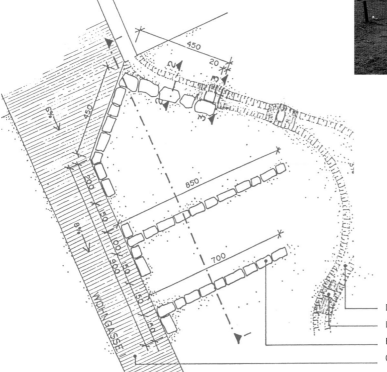

Drainage trench
Level change
Blocks of Ruhr limestone
Concrete pavement

Car parking

Public park

Green tongues

General plan of the estate
with the public green area,
which runs seamlessly into
the private green tongues
in the middle of the estate.

Open swales

Square

Open swales

Open swales

Green tongues

Public park

Car parking

Open swales

Retention basin

Meadow with fruit trees

# Sewage treatment plant at the Wörme Hofgemeinschaft in Handeloh

Decentralized purification
plants are particularly
suitable for remote farms
and hamlets in country
areas.

Fitting the sheet seal in
a purification bed. Here
laymen can help as well –
a school class at work.

Setting the manholes
and introducing the
filter substrate

Installing the substrate
for a purification bed
layer by layer

Planting the beds
with aquatic plants
(phragmitis)

»O'er seven stones the water flows, 'tis pure again, the farmer knows.« This piece of agricultural wisdom may well no longer apply to the present day and the highly complex ways in which water is now polluted, but there is a grain of truth in it: water is able to purify itself. Nothing has changed here. But cities have long since had to say goodbye to giving sewage the time and space to purify itself. They have ultimately arrived at narrow-mesh sewerage networks and treatment plants, via the intermediate stage of evil-smelling sewage farms. This is a hygienic but very expensive method of getting rid of the daily quota of faeces.

Since the early nineties, country people have increasingly started to remember decentralized sewage treatment. An increasing number of farmers, but also private householders who have enough land, are letting their sewage flow not over seven stones, but through settling tanks and purification beds, so that it can then pass into an effluent tank having been cleaned. This also applies to the Hofgemeinschaft in Wörme, an organic farm in Handeloh, south of Hamburg. The Dreiseitl studio planned a sewage treatment plant for about 30 people who live there plus holiday visitors and participants in educational projects.

The planners took advantage of the natural slope on the site, and were thus able to do without technical units to a large extent. Thus sewage from the farm first flows into a 250 metre long collector tank and then into three shafts. Here a filter sack separates solid and liquid components. Alternate use of the shafts means that the contents of the filled bags can be pre-composted and used in fields and gardens after nine to fifteen months.

The liquid part then flows into purification beds with an area of seven square metres per resident equivalent. The botanical treatment plant is de-

The decentralized treatment plant with purification beds treats all the sewage from the hamlet of Unterbach, which has 80 inhabitants.

Residents can service the plant themselves, as it is easy to manage; this gives people long-term responsibility for their own sewage disposal.

Sewage treatment for an agricultural establishment with nursery

signed for a maximum of 100 resident equivalents. The sewage runs through the beds in two stages: first of all through four 80 centimetre deep beds arranged in parallel, with a infiltration length of five metres. In the second stage the beds are one metre deep with a infiltration length of seven metres. The plants that grow there introduce considerable quantities of oxygen into the earth- or water-bearing layer. Aerobic decomposition processes are then set in train. After passing the sampling shaft the purified sewage runs into the little river Seeve via a semi-natural channel with plants growing in it. Very little care and maintenance has proved to be necessary. The purification beds have simply to be kept free of undesirable vegetation and woody plants. The pipes and gutters have to be flushed out three to four times a year to test and maintain their ability to function.

The plant has been working without problems, economically and without complaint since 1994. The Wörme farm's treatment plant has thus contributed to regional water quality, but also considerably reinforced its image as an organic farm and seminar venue.

The sewage seeps through several planted tanks and harmful substances are removed by organic decomposition processes at the various purification stages.

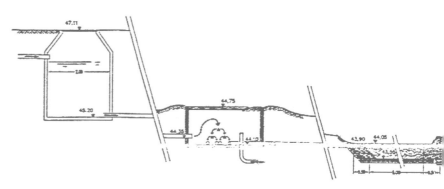

Section through the various purification stages: sewage flows horizontally through plant filters.

Mechanical purification stage          Distribution manhole 1          Biological purification, stage 1

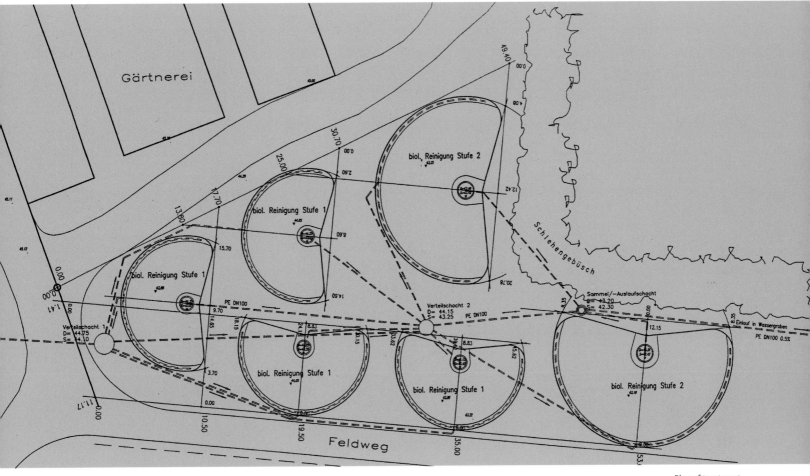

Plan of treatment
plant with various
purification beds

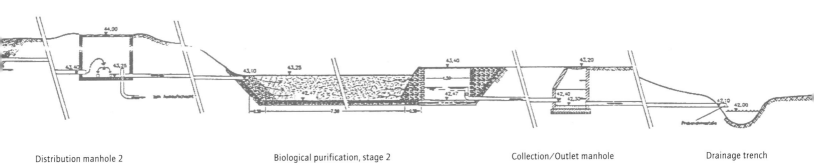

Distribution manhole 2        Biological purification, stage 2        Collection/Outlet manhole        Drainage trench

# Scheme for the banks of the Volme, Hagen

There are some towns that have a considerable number of inhabitants and whose names are familiar, but do not trigger any associations. For example, you've heard of Hagen, but it's unlikely that you can describe more than the platform on the InterCity line. It's the same with rivers. The Ennepe is familiar enough, but how many people know that it flows into the Volme, which is a tributary of the Ruhr? Only people who live in Hagen, you might think. Anyway, the rivers come together just outside the town gates, and the Volme runs through the town centre.

But in the case of Hagen's inhabitants you can't even be certain about the Volme. As in many other places, this town with 200,000 inhabitants at the southern gateway of the Ruhr has treated its river somewhat shabbily. It was downgraded to a canal in the past hundred years, polluted with industrial waste and hidden away behind factory halls. The municipal backyards are all on the Volme. For this reason the town brought its angry citizens into the equation when it was choosing a site for its new town hall on the Volme. The people voted to dump these plans in a local referendum – until they heard in autumn 2000 about the idea of making the river and above all its banks attractive to the population at this point. At the same time the open-space planners wanted to lay the foundation stones for a waterway redevelopment that was to be continued in the long term. For example, the bottoms of the waterways were to be roughened, two weirs were to be removed or at least lowered, and banks arranged to impede the water or to allow it to flow.

As the concrete bed is slowly crumbling away, a complete change of direction is being contemplated for the imminent redevelopment.

Model of first design ideas

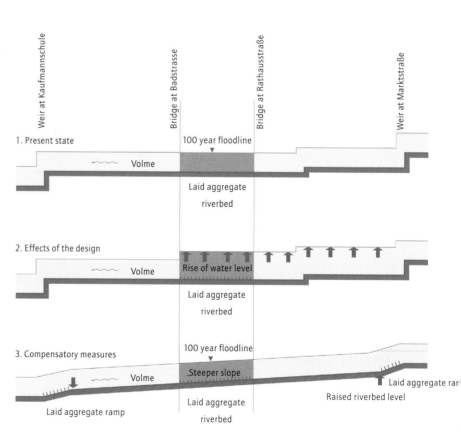

Hydraulic assessment of the present state of the Volme and projected effects of a new design

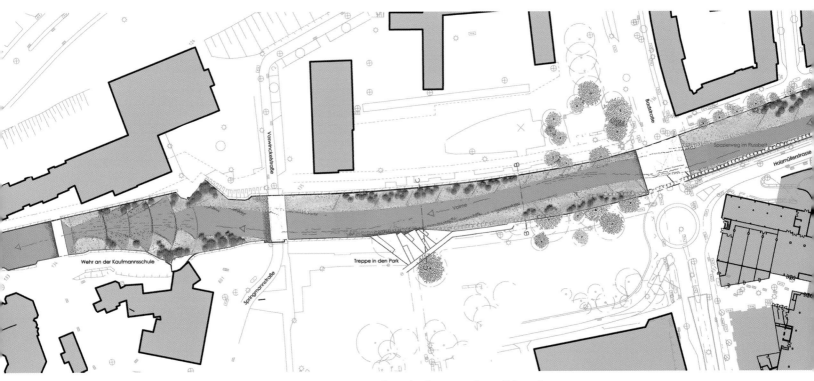

General plan for the town hall area with complete redesign of the river bed and the water features by the town hall. A crucial feature of the design is to restore accessibility for flora and fauna by rebuilding two weirs.

But the people of Hagen seemed most impressed by suggestions for designing the area between the town hall and the Volme. A terrace is to curve along the bank of the river, with enough room for bistro chairs, jutting out over the water in places. From this terrace, a generously dimensioned flight of steps will lead down to the gravel shore, and from there it will be possible to walk to the next steps. Unless the path is flooded when the river is high. Then a narrow pedestrian bridge will lead from the terrace to the other side of the river. But in Hagen, Herbert Dreiseitl also has to meet the challenge of creating a visible link between the future town hall and the river. He intends to do this with inlays set in the floor covering and leading to a water-wall made of coloured glass, down which water will glide. This will be the starting-point for a water-course that will take water from the roof and take it in a cascade down the steps into the Volme.

To make the terrace and steps part of the town, to remove its backyard image and to give people easier access to the

Volme, the floor covering will be taken on into the adjacent street. Even if all this will not really make a great deal of difference to how well people know this industrial town – it will certainly enhance the quality of life of the people who live there.

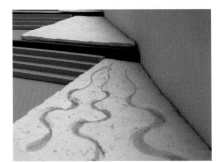

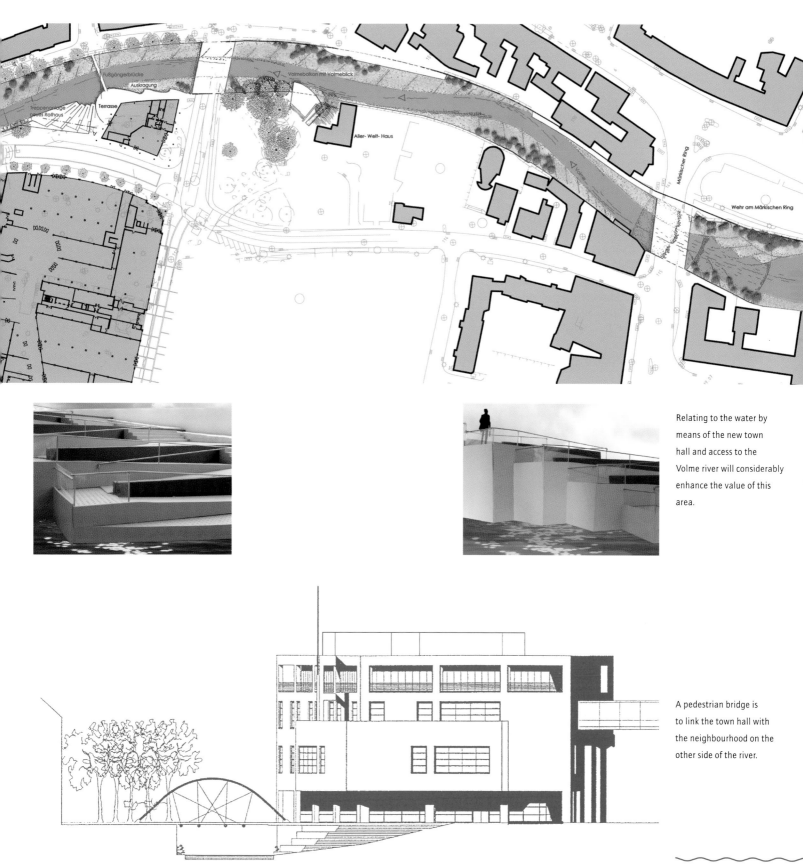

Relating to the water by means of the new town hall and access to the Volme river will considerably enhance the value of this area.

A pedestrian bridge is to link the town hall with the neighbourhood on the other side of the river.

# Green roof for Chicago City Hall

The flat roof of the historic city hall in downtown Chicago is to be transformed into a green roof garden.

Many people are familiar with the riveting view from the Empire State Building in Manhattan. Skyscrapers as far as the eye can see, the Hudson River blurs into the horizon, a freedom-loving, copper-clad lady 46 metres high becomes tiny. But at some point the far distance becomes boring and the eye finds its way back and looks down at apparently trivial details: yellow taxis, for example, the winding paths taken by individuals, clouds of pigeons suddenly flying up, the upward and downward staggered patchwork quilt of the flat roofs. Flat roofs are very popular in big American cities. Unlike Central Europe, the airy space in these little rectangles is used for air-conditioning units and fresh water tanks, sometimes for junk. You would look pretty much in vain for a roof garden here. The USA is still a developing country when it comes to roof planting.

Fewer people know the view from the Sears Tower in Chicago, one of the highest office buildings in the world, but if you look down from there it looks quite like the Manhattan roofscape. But this could change very soon, as this great city on Lake Michigan is one of the five major American cities taking part in the environment authority's »Urban Heat Island Initiative« pilot project. This is the United States' attempt to reduce temperatures in the summer months, which are sometimes very high, and the smog levels in several cities. Roof planting is one of the key elements of this programme, which is also intended to relieve the overloaded sewers when the rainfall is heavy.

There are very few roof-planting experts in the USA because of lack of experience. For this reason the Dreiseitl studio was invited to join an American planning team in 1999, and commissioned to produce a design for a roof area of about 3,600 square metres. And so now people look down from the top of the nearby skyscrapers on to the roof of the eleven-storey town hall. The walls below it are over a hundred years old, and familiar to European film fans at least as the notorious Blues Brothers paid their debts there at the last minute.

What has emerged on top of the town hall is a lightly contoured landscape, planted on a shallow substrate with varieties of sedum and on a deeper one with trees and shrubs. It is possible to walk around the city hall roof on a curving path. Parts of the roof were removed for statical reasons before the planting, and provision of water for the roof plants was dealt with as part of this process. Rainwater from the penthouse (for technical units) which is built directly on to city hall, and higher, is stored in several small tanks and taken to the plants when needed. If water is short, the municipal supply can be used.

City hall's green roof has attracted a great deal of attention, and as part of the environment authority's pilot project it has interested specialists, even outside Chicago. In the city itself it is part of the extensive »City Roof Garden Program«, and the first example of the fact that planting on roofs is worthwhile, even from the point of view of economical and sustainable water management.

The planned garden will be visible from the surrounding skyscrapers and can thus become a visual highlight.

Building work showing the fitting of the roof sealing strips, drainage layers and intermediate layers

The roof garden
under construction

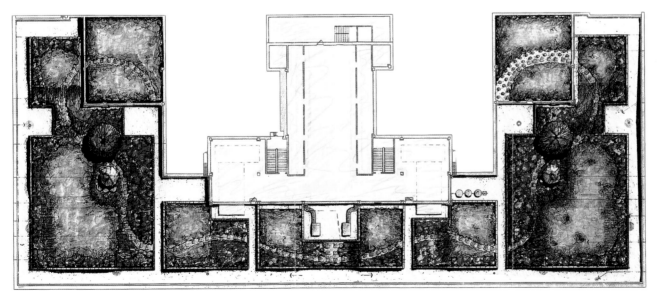

Design for the planted
roof: the individual areas
form a coherent roof garden.

# The Lanferbach at Schüngelberg estate in Gelsenkirchen

Formerly a sewer with sheet-pile walls, the Lanferbach now runs by the Schüngelberg estate in a leisurely fashion.

Before it was redesigned the Lanferbach was forced into a concrete corset and ran through a fenced-off area – »Danger – No Entry« was the order of the day.

Overflow of one of the overgrown infiltration swales

The steps by the bed of the stream invite people to stay for a while and play. An old brick wall was used for their construction.

Most of the planners from elsewhere had to get used to two things over the ten years of the International Building Exhibition at Emscher Park: first to the stock of language that had emerged in Germany's melting pot, borrowing all kinds of vocabulary that would otherwise be unfamiliar from the various immigrant groups. And to a kind of person that does not take at lot of things particularly seriously. For example, all the tillefitt, or fuss, about the IBA. Many of these have still not realized that a building exhibition took place in the Ruhr at all, and that countless projects were completed or considered that had a great deal of influence on the local people's living conditions. It is only when your own front garden has been decontaminated or an almost completely natural stream appears instead of a concrete drainage gutter that even the people who didn't particularly care – it was all »six of one« or »jacket or trousers«, as the German expression has it – that the landscape had taken a turn for the better. It is possible to walk around in it again, to experience it.

One project that became known well beyond the boundaries of the Ruhr is in Gelsenkirchen. A Jugendstil estate in front of the giant Rungenberg spoil heap, also known as Mount Slag, was redeveloped and tastefully complemented with slender terraced housing. The Schüngelberg housing estate for miners had previously been grey, surrounded by dismal green, and bordered by an open, evil-smelling sewer. After redevelopment the complex felt completely different – also helped by attractive open spaces. These appear in the form of nicely proportioned streets, attractive gardens and above all a park which came into being as part of a new rainwater concept. The Lanferbach had previously been a canalized stream in which contaminated water from the Rungenberg slag heap flowed towards the river Emscher. Today the liquid

Site management in the mud of Monte Schlacko

99

Infiltration swale under construction. Water started to accumulate here even in the building phase.

Street water is filtered and purified in retention basins that are inte-grated into the design, then fed underground to the stream.

Along with the Rungenberg slag heap, which has now been planted, the Lanferbach now functions as a coherent public park area, and is used by the residents for all kinds of activities.

poison flows out of a collective drain into a sewer. This opened up the way for water management in which rainwater from the Schüngelberg estate flows first through various purification stages and retention basins, and is then released in a controlled way into the restored and completely redesigned Lanferbach. Street water runs straight into the retention basins by the Lanferbach and seeps towards the stream through water-bearing strata.

A valuable biotope will develop along a length of just under eight hundred metres, but this is not all. In fact the estate residents have acquired a new park, which is used a great deal, especially by the large proportion of Turkish inhabitants. Steps intended as seats, built of re-used bricks, draw austere lines in the otherwise gently contoured park landscape. These are the meeting places, which are reached via winding pathways that adapt to the natural design of the park. And the final benefit from the new design is that existing harmful waste was disposed of safely, which at least for the residents of the Schüngelberg estate is not schissko-jedno – which is derived from the Polish wszystko jedno, and means roughly the same as »jacket or trousers«.

The bridge over the Lanferbach with its discreetly designed steps links the Schüngelberg, the Lanferbach and the Rungenberg slag heap.

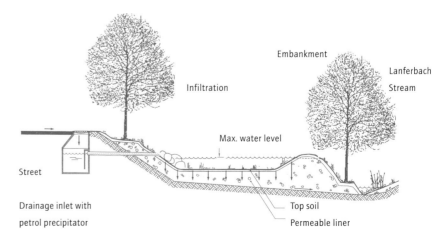

Infiltration

Embankment

Lanferbach Stream

Max. water level

Street

Drainage inlet with petrol precipitator

Top soil

Permeable liner

# Housing estate in Echallens near Lausanne

The meandering channel is in the central square in the estate, and shows the history of the course of a river with changing loops. At the end a rhythmically pulsating movement is set up that is reminiscent of organic forms (John Wilkes' Flowforms).

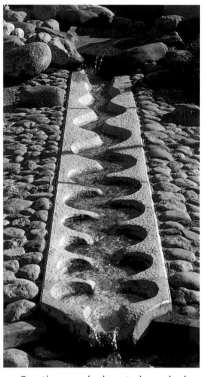

Creative people do not always look back on their early work with particular pleasure. We sometimes hear that the artist is pleased to have developed further. This implies an admission that time passes by one's own work as well, that it is subject to fashion – even when designing open space. But ultimate artists are content to know that every work is a step along a path, without which it would not have been possible to reach one's current position – and this alone means that every work is valid in its own right. And as well as this it is enjoyable to see the effect of earlier projects on the thinking of a whole profession, and even on related ones.

This may well be the case for the Dreiseitl studio and the Hameau de la Fontaine estate project in Echallens. In the early eighties, surface water drainage, swale infiltration, purification in reed beds, installing underground cisterns and re-using rainwater were all seen as newfangled ideas in urban development that people were a little suspicious of. And so it was all the more courageous of the people of Echallens

near Lausanne to commit themselves to an experiment by using a modern rainwater management idea for an estate with ninety dwellings. Since 1986, all the surface water here has flowed along the streets in gutters to a sealed treatment bed. Here the roots of reeds and rushes, in symbiosis with the filter floor, remove the harmful substances from the water before some of it runs into storage tanks. From here water is pumped to the central village well, which is a meeting-place, but also a sculpture, whose impressive volume of flowing water sets currents in motion, whose veil of water reacts to wind, and that is perhaps reminiscent of the fact that the source of all life once sprang from the village fountain. As well as this, a play and adventure area draws its water supply from the tanks. The rest of the rainwater flows into a retention pond, where it evaporates, soaks away or is fed slowly into a stream. The presence of delicate amphibians in the form of alpine salamanders and palmated newts demonstrates the high quality of the water from the reed and rush basins, and also show the importance of artificial water features as second-hand survival biotopes.

It was clear from a very early stage in the Hameau de la Fontaine that how the disciplines of art, open-space architecture, leisure research and environmental technology fuse together to form a single theme.

The centre of the village with a treatment biotope under a platform that is available for performances.

Paved basins show how the rainwater drains away.

Here a second-hand biotope becomes a habitat for creatures under threat, in this case an alpine salamander.

The fountain with its watercourse is a special feature of this estate.

A naturally designed retention pond forms the edge of the estate.

# Rainwater management in Krems Business Park, Austria

At times when flooding is on the increase, local authorities think about the omissions of recent years and decades. And they have to do this, as the damage caused by water in recent years have became a regular item in the accounts of local authorities, cantons and states. Unfortunately it is not until it gets difficult to balance the books that ready arguments are available for taking new directions in water management. And here it is important not to be too morose about having to do today what one could have wanted to do yesterday.

The Lower Austrian town of Krems an der Donau demonstrated this in terms of rainwater management. Here the municipal engineers drew up estimates for draining a proposed 33 hectare industrial estate with a conventional sewerage system. But before the community started to implement this, it was well advised to have an alternative concept devised, for open rainwater management. This produced pleasing results. It was possible to use infiltration techniques even for an industrial area in the Danube catchment area with relatively high groundwater levels. Of course the gravelly, sandy subsoil with a Kf value of $1 \times 10^{-3}$ was of considerable

assistance here. The director of building was particularly pleased when he was able to show a financial saving of over 50 % against the proposed costs for the sewerage solution.

The technical framework for this success lies in a system of long swale strips along the main access road, and infiltration basins between the buildings. Alongside the main access road, the yard and parking areas drain into the decentralized gravel trenches, each complete in itself, after passing through light-density material separators. There are planted retention basins above the trenches. Once the water has arrived here it soaks through a treatment layer about 50 centimetres thick into the gravel trench, which is clad in shear wool, and runs from there into the ground. Roof water flows into planted soakaway basins, and from there into the groundwater. All the sewage is fed into a separate sewer and taken to the communal sewage treatment plant. A relatively large number of roof gardens definitely contribute to the overall efficiency of the concept. Rainwater is delayed in draining from about a third of the buildings. The effects of open infiltration are best studied when rainfall is heavy. The industrial estate has

canals running through it from which water occasionally runs over the edges on to the lawns – but without getting as far as the buildings. But the Landesdorfer Arm, which is linked directly with the Danube, maintains a water level that is well under the top of the embankment. The Krems East industrial estate does not contribute a drop to possible flooding on the Danube and its tributaries.

Constructing a swale system between parking spaces

Gaps in the kerb allow rainwater to run off the streets into the grassed swale alongside and seep away there.

Infiltration via open joints in the pavement

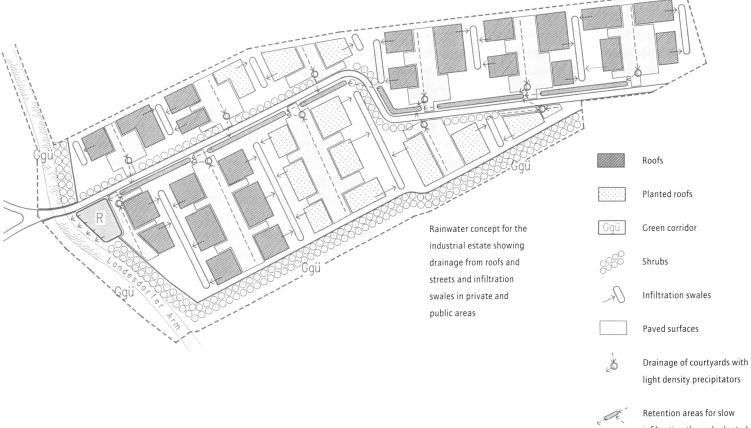

Rainwater concept for the industrial estate showing drainage from roofs and streets and infiltration swales in private and public areas

| | |
|---|---|
| 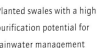 | Roofs |
| | Planted roofs |
| Ggü | Green corridor |
| | Shrubs |
| | Infiltration swales |
| | Paved surfaces |
| | Drainage of courtyards with light density precipitators |
| 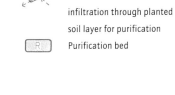 | Retention areas for slow infiltration through planted soil layer for purification |
| R | Purification bed |

A retention basin with infiltration after heavy rain

Grassed swales are placed next to the parking spaces, the trees planted there flourish even in the conditions prevailing in locations of this kind.

Planted swales with a high purification potential for rainwater management

# Water as an open system

Wolfram Schwenk

**Water is by nature formless and passive, and only shows its particular qualities when interacting with its surroundings. These qualities constitute its significance in the context of nature and teach us to handle water correctly.**

Water has become a museum exhibit recently. This gives me pause for thought, as generally speaking museums concern themselves with things that are not (any longer) part of people's everyday experience. And now water in its natural diversity falls into this category, which for me is eloquent evidence of man's alienation from the elemental basis of his life.

We banish water from our environment and allow it to appear for certain purposes only. And so we only perceive it out of context, in specific functions: as a medium between tap and sink, as a drink in a bottle, as rain in the street, as sewage in a sewer, as an attraction in a museum, and in recent years as a flood as well. The links, common to all, archetypal, water's context and its significance in nature are foreign to us. And yet we are talking about the most important basis of our existence, which cannot be replaced by anything else – and not about any old raw material or cultural factor.

Deliberately drawing attention to water has become a cultural activity that would have been difficult to imagine in earlier days. The following remarks about some of water's characteristics are offered to this end.

When trying to describe water using everyday concepts we are immediately confronted with an unexpected problem: as a liquid, water has no shape of its own. It is formless and unconfined, has no hardness or sound of its own – not metallic, not wooden, not bright, not dull. It also has no colour of its own, no smell, no taste of its own.

We also cannot also understand water fully with our five senses: all these can tell us is what it is not and what it doesn't have. And so just as it runs away between our fingers it runs away between our definitions. This is a challenge to reflect and to rethink.

**No shape of its own:** If water is placed in a container it fills it up and adopts its shape. At the top it always ends as a free waterlevel that adjusts itself to the parallel with the ideal horizon, the surface of the earth. It adapts to its surroundings, down to its very form. If you tilt the vessel, the surface of the water remains horizontal – unlike fixed bodies, whose form is retained when they are twisted and turned. And so for water its situation, its equilibrium is more important that its form – when it is released, it again tries to create a horizontal surface.

**No hardness of its own:** Water cannot be polished. But you can submerge yourself in it without resistance or throw objects like stones into it. It gives way, accepts these objects and surrounds them.

**No sound of its own:** When pouring water into a tall glass we notice that the colour and pitch of the sound depend on how full the glass is, in other words on the air-space in the cavity. This also applies to the plashing, murmuring and glugging sound of a brook.

**No taste of its own:** And yet it is only the moist film of water on our tongues and in our noses that conveys all the nuances to us. We cannot smell or taste anything if our tongue and nose dry up.

Everything that comes into being or passes away, everything that is combined or separated as a material in nature does so only with the aid of water: substances dissolve in it. »Substances can have an effect only in solution« could be a free re-statement of an old chemical principle. All natural management of substances lives with and on water: in the atmosphere, in the ground, in rocks, and in the waters themselves; in living creatures in breathing and feeding, excretion, regulation, growth, regeneration and reproduction. There is no life without water. Water always mediates, without itself being entirely subsumed in the products of the reactions. It is there to show other things to their best advantage and to convey other things.

As a chemical combination of hydrogen and oxygen, water is defined as $H_2O$. But pure $H_2O$ does not occur in nature, and not even in the laboratory: in its pure chemical form water is such a powerful solvent that it immediately combines with other substances at the moment it comes into being and dissolves and absorbs at least traces of these. Even the substance we call pure water is always more than $H_2O$ – because it is always open to its surroundings, and is always interacting with them. This is why it is so vulnerable and so in need of protection.

If substances go into solution or are watered down they lose their own form and spatial confinement and gradually fill – together with all the other substances dissolved in it – the whole spatial content of the water that is dissolving them. In their dry and solid form they were distinct from each other within their own forms; now these limitations are lifted and the substances can develop their functional chemical qualities and enter into intimate relationships with each other. In the course of this they adopt an almost weightless condition of floating in the water. Weight loss as a result of buoyancy – divers are always disoriented by the equal pressure from all directions when under water – means being exposed to forces coming from all directions in the surrounding area, a universal balance of forces. Water in water is in this universally open condition.

Running water is a material continuum. It behaves as a coherent whole, not as a material made up of individual particles. And so it does not respond to stimuli in isolation, but always as a whole, systemically. Even minimal shifts in the equilibrium of forces within it set water in motion, and make it flow or pour. Starting at the point where this movement was provoked, fast and slow flowing areas mingle. Along curving or often rolling sections this leads to shearing, in other words partly pulling, partly pushing movements, to blockages and eddying in rhythmic sequence.

Set in motion by interplay with its surroundings, water, which is otherwise so passive, surprises us by producing a whole variety of forms like eddies and waves – and as they come into being they also immediately transform themselves. Every change of movement in water causes shapes to be formed and re-formed, and ultimately these flow away into nothing as soon as they become calm. A game that ceaselessly produces something new, transforms it and takes it back again, a continuous process without a lasting result.

In its material quality water is shapeless, it has no form of its own, but dissolves forms and changes them. It is only movement that makes it a design medium, the scene of an inexhaustible process of renewal, with shapes being ceaselessly formed and transformed, coming into being and passing away.

Many of the development stages of flow formation in water are strikingly similar to organic forms: they can be addressed as organic in terms of their forms. The formative movements that lead to the formation of such currents with their blockages and stretching, overlapping and rolling up in sections with a multiplicity of curves, obey the same laws as the formative movements in the embryonic development of organisms. But something that in an organism becomes the apparently durable condition of the form of a body and its organs through an equilibrium of flow between ceaseless new formation and simultaneous dissolution, remains a formative process in water, and does not acquire a lasting quality. Thus the formative principles of organic and living nature are reproduced as processual events in moving water under the universal conditions of weightlessness and of forces in states that are changing in an unstable fashion. Life-supporting wisdom is woven into these processes. This is – alongside the mediation of metabolism in organisms – the second major sphere in which water works to convey life. Each mingles with the other.

Recent astrophysical research has shown that the laws governing currents in moving water are part of the laws of flow that govern the entire cosmos. The ways the stars relate to each other also follow these laws. And the patterns adopted by the little floating droplets that water forms when falling provide an image of this – they reflect the whole cosmos on a small scale.

In summary: formlessly passive water, mineral according to its material quality, is opened up to the formative forces in living nature by movement. This is shown by the flow patterns that are formed. At the same time they reveal cosmic laws of order: organic laws are also cosmic. The universal laws that form the basis of all life can also be revealed in moving water, and affect it.

Water lives by coming to terms with its surroundings, though excitability, rhythmical articulation in the course of pattern-forming and pattern-changing, and by mediating metabolic processes, and it enlivens those surroundings at the same time.

These qualities of water can be seen in infinite diversity in natural watercourses: in springs and mountain streams it is largely conditions working from the outside – like the structure of the bed, the slope, the daily pattern of light and warmth etc. – that determine the behaviour of water and the absorption and transport of solid and dissolved substances. In big rivers, lakes and in the sea these processes take place to a greater extent inside the masses of water in the form of substance conversion and separation. In meandering streams and rivers on plains these tendencies to absorption, conversion and separation, to shaping and mediating, run in a flow of rhythmical equilibrium. As it comes to terms with the landscape, the course of the river itself becomes an image of these events.

If a creative artist wants to bring about cosmic and organic flow forms in water, this cannot be done in the same way as a sculpture, for example, would be created. They can only be evoked by handling water like an instrument. The creative process then takes place in the water itself. For the artist or designer working with water, this means that he or she makes only part of the work of art. The other, livelier part has to be left to the water – it is to the water that the completion of the work is entrusted. If the artist has learned how water twists and turns as it flows, how it eddies, trickles and spurts, flies and builds up, surges and sloshes, rests and reflects, then some of this can be enhanced and emphasized by creative design, and made into the theme of the joint work of art. Then the designer or artist is working in partnership with the water. This stimulates observers to become aware of the special qualities of water, to discover and experience it, to love it and to value it – and so to learn how to treat it carefully. I know of no better, more attractive and more sustainable ecological study course than this!

A transparent platform for spectators. The use of light and water is carefully calculated, and here the individual phenomena and phases are being staged. Suddenly the old wooden gutters under the platform are flooded.

Veils of mist and vapour in the light. Here we are able to see the relationship between the ways in which air and water move.

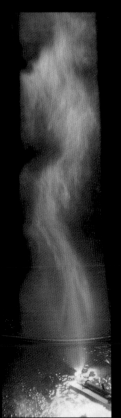

Natural processes are repeated daily without our knowing exactly what is happening. Do we have a sudden moment of insight when looking at the morning mist or a rainbow, do we know why a drop falls of a leaf at a particular time, and not a moment earlier or later? Unfortunately, being uncertain does not always trigger a thirst for knowledge. Even the most watery problem can sometimes seem too dry, and the chemistry and physics that could explain it are much too complicated. People like to have answers to their questions, but please make them easy to understand and ideally demonstrated in three dimensions.

When Herbert Dreiseitl demonstrated phenomena involving water in the Ruhr city of Gelsenkirchen as part of the Federal Horticultural show in 1997, his intention was to engage and fascinate easy-going people of this kind as well. He found the ideal setting for his experiment in showing water in all its states in a cooling tower that had been left standing at the Nordstern pit. After a fifteen minute introduction a fine film of water had formed on the spectators' hair and clothes – a perfectly harmless way of acquiring the feeling of being in the middle of a rain-cloud. What had happened? The spectators stood on a glass mezzanine floor, and the development from mist to a cloudburst was played out before their eyes, with every step in the process accompanied by gigantic slide projections. Every sense was working overtime as first of all their was nothing to be seen in the dark interior of the cooling tower, and then only indirect light, with a bank of mist moving ponderously into position in front of it. Turbulence on the periphery made shining droplets form dancing figures. Slides of foggy landscape thrust into this moving image. Then a circular

The old cooling tower, a relic of the former Goldstern pit in Gelsenkirchen, was the scene for a unique presentation of water-related phenomena for over two years.

The magic world of water vapour in an experiment in the old cooling tower

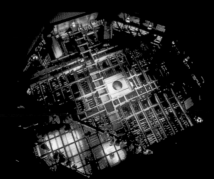

Spectators' stand, slatted frame and the fittings involved in this magical installation

Spectators on the stand
looking up as if spell-bound,
something is going on …

movement. Followed by more rings, it rose to the top of the cooling tower in a cone of light, and then faded away in an air current, along with the clouds of mist. The slide projections of cloud formations appeared on the wall of the cooling tower – there was rain in the air. And it started to fall, first as drizzle, split up into numerous colour zones by beams of light, and then crashing down as an impressive cloudburst. Towards the end the projector revealed another detail: a huge drop of water was getting ready to fall, changing its shape in the first phase of detachment and flight. The demonstration ended with slides of roaring waterfalls – but admittedly not without returning to the cooling tower's original function. The glass platform allowed visitors to see part of the old system of gutters below them filling with water, which then dripped down on to the slatted structure below. Finally we saw how the slats worked to bring about air cooling and make the cooling tower work: the drops of water atomize as they impact, which means that a greater surface area of the water is exposed to the air. The heat in the water is largely dispersed by a stream of air generated by thermal currents, which warms up. It's as simple as that.

The Dreiseitl studio was able to repeat the performance in the IBA presentation year, 1999. The city of Gelsenkirchen wanted to find a long-term operator for the tower – until it was destroyed by arsonists in autumn 2000.

A circular eddy starts to rise from the depths of the cooling tower.

Vapour, mist and smoke remind us of natural and industrial phenomena in the Ruhr.

Spectators can follow the presentation from the glass platform.

Veils of rain and drizzle dance in an air-current in the illuminated cooling tower.

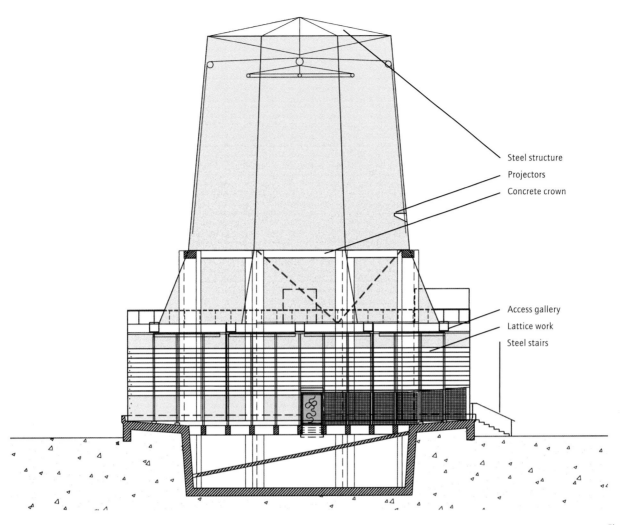

Steel structure
Projectors
Concrete crown

Access gallery
Lattice work
Steel stairs

Elevation and plan
of the cooling tower

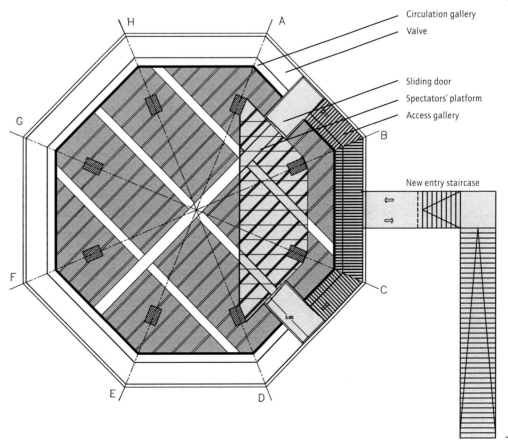

Circulation gallery
Valve

Sliding door
Spectators' platform
Access gallery

New entry staircase

H    A

G

F

E    D    C    B

3.95

111

# Healing garden in Königsfeld

Rainwater stored in a tank is fed into the flowing water through a bronze sculpture.

Things that are scarcely imaginable to some people are matters of long, tried-and-tested experience for others. This is a phenomenon that one comes across frequently in the field of alternative medicine – and an example is foot reflex therapy. Ancient cultures like those of China, India or Egypt and that of the original inhabitants of America knew that the whole man could be treated in the »microsystem« of the feet. But as in other matters as well, this wisdom had to make its way across the American continent before it was accepted in Europe. First of all the North American Indians passed on the healing and strengthening powers of foot reflex zone massage to their white conquerors, and finally these insights filtered through into German textbooks: human energy centres are accessible from the soles of the feet.

A leading European practitioner in this field is Hanne Marquardt, who has now made a name with a recognized method of her own, and is based in a teaching centre in Königsfeld. A garden covering two hundred square metres was created for this training establishment on the western fringes of the Black Forest in 1990. The course members can relax here between seminars, but they can also get to know the soles of their feet as a source of experience. For this reason the garden addresses the notion of walking in bare feet. Visitors can derive a number of sensual impressions from a variety of surfaces, with dry feet and in water. It is the unfamiliar and varied sensations conveyed by the bottoms of the pools and streams in particular that vastly broaden the horizon of experience. Guests can walk on warm granite slabs and sandy paths, and wade in refreshing water over gravel and wade, supported by a handrail, through paved basins containing deeper water. They get to know the water and the ground through the sense of touch in their feet.

Various water arteries run through the garden, sometimes shallow, sometimes collecting in metre-deep pools, then there are stepping stones in the bed of a stream, and then sometimes it splashes out of a slender metal sculpture, and sometimes pulsates in floating pools. Warm colours, a mosaic of little spaces and an inclination to run wild are the key features of this sloping garden – and they make it seem considerably larger than it actually is. The wide range of herbaceous perennials makes its own contribution to this.

The foot reflex zone massage garden – various different stone and gravel structures can be explored and felt, some of them under water.

The therapeutic garden – areas for rest and recreation are provided right by the water.

The water helps to shape a herb garden on several levels and washes around small sitting areas.

A little stream runs over flowforms into a pool that is framed by flowering herbs and bushes.

# Fountain sculpture in Immenstaad

The sculpture is put in place.

Design sketch:
The sculpture was
cast in bronze.

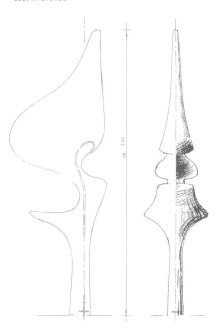

The natural stone steles
are arranged radially.

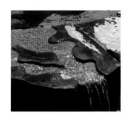

The individual natural
stones reveal wonderful,
artistically developed
shapes that channel
the water.

Arrival and departure – moving moments in man's path through life. And they are particularly striking when there is clearly a long distance ahead of or behind the traveller. Here a town on the sea or a large lake makes coming home or going away most emotional, as one arrives or leaves by ship with deliberation, in the true sense of the word. And there is always a long distance before or behind somebody, in which only water can wash away the last traces.

In Germany, Lake Constance in particular, the country's largest expanse of fresh water, can give the experience of a reasonably long trip by boat. Numerous places on the German, Swiss and Austrian shores receive and say farewell to their residents and visitors – but only a few of them have imposing landmarks to catch the eye. Immenstaad on the north shore used to be one of these. Here the lake widens out to the south-east to the part of it known as the Sea of Baden, and Immenstaad, on a small northern bay, looks south to the majestic chain of the Alps. Over two million people a year embark and disembark here.

Since 1991 they have been taking a bearing on a landmark, meeting at a particular place or leaving the little town looking back at a sculpture that is meant to be unforgettable. A landmark on the landing pier, made of stone, bronze and water. A bronze figure 4.5 metres high grows up out of twelve upright stones, local Dornbirn glauconite and Rohrschach sandstone. It faces south, and forms a sensitive point at which the forces of sun, water and wind seem to be concentrated. Its gesture is open to interpretation: water, falling and atomizing according to the strength of the wind gives it a sense of lightness, and can transform rigid metal into a waving flag. It points to the sky, stands in the water, and mediates between the two.

Seen with the horizontal
breadth of the lake – with
the Swiss Alps in the background – the fountain
provides a vertical landmark.

The water collects in a large stepped roundel and then flows, regulated by weirs if necessary, through channels and back into Lake Constance.

On the land side the fountain runs radially in the form of natural stone steles placed on a bed of river pebbles. The location needs a scale of about three hundred square metres to develop its full symbolic power and range of uses. »Free man in the elemental universe« is Herbert Dreiseitl's name for his bronze sculpture. We can believe this – or something completely different. And it is also possible to have different ideas about using the sculpture. The ensemble as a whole is not meant to be just a landmark. It has certainly become a popular meeting-point and place to spend some time. Children like to climb around the steles, and play in the water among the drainage channels with their little weirs, and to use the gravel bed as an area for their own excursions. Adults join in the games, work out the flow patterns of the water on sculpted steles or lose themselves in the visual interplay of distance and proximity. When the lake floods parts of the fountain when the snow melts in summer people are reminded of things that are happening beyond the sculpture, in the far distance. Perhaps a boat is departing for that destination.

Children find little weirs
that can be used to regulate
the flow of the water back
into Lake Constance.

The water and wind
sculpture in a föhn storm

The lake undergoes dynamic changes in its water level, and so parts of the sculpture disappear with the seasons and then reappear.

The fountain from above. Its radial basic shape is continued in individual stone blocks on the shore of Lake Constance.

# documenta urbana in Kassel

The city of Kassel has been staging the documenta urbana every four to five years since 1955. Numerous artists who have become world famous attracted international attention for the first time at this exhibition, giving a new impetus to fine art and addressing exciting tasks for the future.

In 1984, documenta also addressed the theme of living together in cities. At that time ecological questions about building were being asked for the first time, and these are now used by numerous cities to set the standards for their development plans. Particular attention was paid in this case to rainwater management, which made heavy demands on the handling of open space – a problem that was solved in an exemplary fashion in 1984, in a new district called »In der Dönke«, which was built by several distinguished architects. The Dreiseitl studio took on various landscape planning tasks, along with the Hamburg landscape architect Raimund Herms, and was responsible for the water concept in particular. The planners accorded rainwater, which is usually just a nuisance, an artistic dimension of its own. For example, Raimund Herms used his paving work, which has become a trademark in the meantime, to make paths and squares into promenade artworks, in which everything seemed to be in a state of flux. Herbert Dreiseitl literally captured the surface water, then fed it via open channels through paths and pedestrian areas into extensive retention ponds – and into the full view of the passers-by. The water is purified by the symbiotic interplay of rhizomes and micro-organisms and constant addition of oxygen by the use of flowform basins. In Kassel water can be experienced immediately. Children soon announced that these watercourses and the flowform cascade were their favourite places to play, residents relaxed by the densely planted pools, which purified themselves in this way,

Flowing patterns in the different pavement materials correspond to the flowing movement of the water.

and insects and amphibians that have no chance of survival in most settlements increased their numbers. Fences were not needed because of the shallow embankment contours.

Residents are a good yardstick for the quality of urban environments. They, and young people in particular, still make intensive use of this extensive and varied landscape. The open-air concept has proved its worth.

Retention ponds with reed zones as purification areas form an attractive transition at the end of the town.

A little stream is supplied by a circulation system and thus contributes to improving the water quality.

Children playing freely where they can discover water

# »Dunsthöhle« and main avenue in Bad Pyrmont

Stainless steel bubbles symbolize gas being emitted from, the »Dunsthöhle« on the approach to the site, as its identifying feature. They can be played on, occupied and balanced on by adults and children.

A structured, dark wall with a chink exuding mist, as a fountain and a suggestion of faults and the phenomenon of gas being emitted from the subsoil.

The city of Hanover acquired a world-wide reputation, at least for six months. A small town seventy kilometres to the south-west, in the foothills of the Weserbergland, also enjoys a world-wide reputation and can look back on a remarkable tradition at World Fairs. The little town featured in the Chicago World Fair as long ago as 1893, telling the story of a sensational well discovery there, and the tale of its own salvation, which was already 1,800 years old at the time. The little town acquired a world-wide reputation with nine healing springs, a mud bath and carbon dioxide springs, which finally led to public recognition as a spa in 1914.

So Bad Pyrmont owes its fame and wealth to water, greatly enhanced by unique geological formations. Like the town, the historical spa park, which is esteemed just as highly, has been in a constant state of change. It went through the latest one for Expo 2000, by registering as a decentralized location for the World Fair. The theme: water – health, myth and visions.

One myth hovers over the so-called »Dunsthöhle«, or vapour cave, which does not seem to promise anything very healthy at first. Quarry workers were occasionally suffocated in the early 18th century when mining variegated sandstone – which crippled the business, presented the prominent doctor Johann Philipp Seip with a puzzle and gave the quarry the haunting nickname »Dunsthöhle«. In 1775 the heavy gas that was being emitted was identified as carbon dioxide, but it was not used in a carbon dioxide dry gas bath until 1950. The cave itself slipped out of the public eye.

The area around the vapour cave was lit for the Expo event and completely redesigned. New paths were made to it, hornbeam hedges suggest faultlines and provide new structures. An amphitheatre serves as a playground and meeting-place, surrounds the $CO_2$ spring in its semicircular pavilion and

The amphitheatre at the
»Dunsthöhle« – presenting
a natural phenomenon

Path

Meadow

Mistwall

Entrance

Sunken spheres

Dunsthöhle

The park around the
»Dunsthöhle« has been lit
and planted with lines of
hedges relating to fault lines
in the ground, and thus a
reminder of the origins of
the spring phenomenon.

Transparent light and sound devices are roped into the tops of trees in the main avenue, with integrated loudspeakers for the sound-space experience.

draws visitors' attention to the spring itself. Stainless steel spheres set in the site are reminiscent of rising bubbles. These spheres are also a striking feature of the access area on the town centre side. Here they rise out of the ground near to a 120 centimetre high wall in black concrete. But the wall makes sense here as a dark backdrop for a mist fountain whose water vapour suggests the phenomenon of the spring and creates a magical atmosphere, especially when illuminated at night.

In the Expo year, the Dreiseitl studio, working with the Swiss sound artist Andreas Bossard, also installed a very special sound space. Transparent light and sound units were suspended in the central avenue of limes in Bad Pyrmont, thus pointing inventively but subtly to the town's historical importance. Giant drops of water swing through the avenue, so that visitors can find their way by familiar noises in the evening; back into times when spas were something that only the rich could afford and Pyrmont was already famous.

You can hear hackney carriages rattling over the paving-stones – as it might have been at the time when Peter the Great was treated here, or Goethe spent time in Bad Pyrmont and conducted experiments in the »Dunsthöhle«.

Drops swoop through the avenue, dance from tree to tree and open up a new way of looking at this historic Baroque complex.

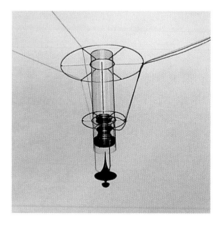

# Towards a new water culture

**Detlev Ipsen**

**We are going to have to learn how to handle water in future. This means co-operative planning and a high level of participation. A project in Hannoversch Münden has produced some early experience in this field.**

If you ask people about environmental problems in surveys, water is almost never mentioned. More of them are aware of traffic, noise and air pollution and the hole in the ozone layer. We carried out surveys in Dresden and Frankfurt in which only 7.6% of the Dresden residents questioned mentioned water as an environmental problem, and in Frankfurt it was only 3.3%. We need to drink water every day, and use it to keep clean, to promote a sense of well-being, and for recreation. So why is it not watched with particular care in respect to possible environmental problems? How can this be explained?

Obviously the fact that water is generally and constantly available, naturally and through technology, the frequent precipitation in our latitudes, full streams and rivers, and running water in our homes all seem to give the lie to the idea that water could be a problem. Anyone who looks at the world a little more closely knows how the deserts are spreading, remembers the droughts in the Sahel and Somalia, and has heard about conflicts over the waters of the Jordan and the Euphrates. But why should water be a problem in Central Europe?

In fact the water problem in Europe is not a problem of quantity, as a rule, even though water represents the greatest flow of any material through our cities. The principal problem in Central Europe is not a general shortage, but a shortage of water of outstanding quality, and the pollution of waterways, which goes far beyond the point at which streams or rivers can clean themselves. Obviously in recent decades people have become accustomed to the fact that rivers are not suitable for bathing, or springs for drinking. Even tap water is distrusted. Over 84% of people never or seldom drink water from the tap.

And so the water problem is first and foremost a problem of quality. The quantity problem comes second. Groundwater pollution has accustomed people to the fact that large cities can draw only a tiny proportion of their water from their own territory, and so use supplies from further away. In any case, poor groundwater quality means considerable expense for treating and transporting water, and often triggers regional conflicts. Then pressure groups demand reduction of the quantities drawn and a more sophisticated handling of water.

The current argument runs that anyone who air-conditions offices with best-quality drinking water, cleans cars and flushes toilets with it, is lowering groundwater levels and causing damage frivolously, not as a matter of necessity. Political pressure can be exerted on towns and cities to be more aware and economical in their use of water by articulating the problems in the areas where it is drawn. But why are people not acutely conscious of the problem despite high costs, possible damage and the risk of endangering health?

The search for an answer to this question leads to the issue of the structure of the modern city. Its development began with the cholera epidemics which haunted many European cities in several waves during the 19th century. At this time and also in the wake of major urban planning changes, such as initiated in Paris by Georges Eugène Haussmann, water pipes were installed.

The shock caused by the cholera epidemics has had a far greater effect than containing and controlling the epidemics themselves. The construction of sewerage systems and the piping of drinking water to individual houses and flats, the gradual spread of private toilets, the establishment of public bathing facilities which then also became more widespread in private houses, did not just build up a general culture of hygiene, but fundamentally changed the relationship between the city and its citizens. Many of the vital processes of urban life were put under state control in the course of this development and offered by municipal utilities to citizens as a compulsorily imposed service. This did not just apply to water supply and waste water disposal, but also to food supply in new abattoirs and covered markets built and controlled by the police, waste disposal, voluntary or compulsory health care and state epidemic policies, down to the control of private living conditions by state housing inspectors.

What does all this mean in terms of the way problems are perceived in towns?

Firstly, many aspects of everyday life were withdrawn from civil authority and handed over to state and municipal bureaucracies. The transformation to the civilized modern town was in fact a process of »de-civilization«. Household and neighbourhood responsibilities for water supply and faeces disposal were taken over by bureaucratic institutions.

Secondly, most of the technical and natural side of this process becomes invisible to ordinary citizens. An individual household cannot possibly see where the water comes from and where it runs away to, and the same applies to food and energy. Significant elements of urban life are no longer directly visible. Hence experience of the natural and technical context of urban life is lost, and new experience of this kind cannot be gained. At the same time responsibility for and thus relation to material elements is becoming increasingly disparate, and on the expert plane this cramps the way in which things are seen.

So the water problem extends to two poles: the material side, which presents itself as a threat to the quality of the resource, and the social side, which is categorized by a loss of awareness of the problem. Both poles are very closely connected with the development of the modern city, where a technical administrative infrastructure has been built up so that the city's natural side can be regulated as efficiently as possible. If we see the emergence of this infrastructure as the 19th century's reply to the environmental crises identified at the time, then the perceptual distance from »nature« is the 20th century social consequence of this piece of problem-solving.

We use the concept of »water culture« to relate the various aspects of water, and thus also of water problems, to each other. Usually the idea of culture is linked with the culture business, with theatre and museums, cinema and concerts. It is also used in a quite different sense from day to day. We talk about a cooking culture, or planning culture, and refer disparagingly to an uncultured attitude. Systematically speaking, the idea of culture has an analytical and a normative aspect. We understand culture to be the meanings and senses that permeate one or more realms of the material and social world. When we speak of water culture we are referring to the meanings and senses that relate to water as a material, to water technology, to the aesthetics of water and to the various social ways of dealing with water. But water culture also includes the interpretations and meanings associated with water. The concept of culture helps us to understand the different aspects of water in their relationship with each other. Just as Roman culture was not made up merely of the Latin language and the writings of Seneca, but also of the roads and aqueducts of the Roman Empire, in the same way water culture includes legal standards, water technology, water economics and social ways of handling water in one meaningful relation. So we do not mean that there would not be a water culture today, but that the water culture that is predominant today could be changed if we try to deal with water in a sustainable manner.

We understand sustainable water culture as a »culture of many waters«. Today as a rule the same water is used for making tea, taking a shower or washing the car. A sustainable water culture would have different water available for different purposes. One and the same lot of water will be put to work in different ways in use cascades. Streams in towns will no longer be drainage ditches and sweep faeces and refuse past the sewage treatment plants into the rivers when it is raining heavily. Rivers will be used for irrigation, for bathing, for sport and for recreation, thus enhancing the value of the landscape outside our front doors.

Prices for water and sewerage services have risen considerably more than the average cost of living in recent years. And the new sustainable water culture will not get any cheaper. This will also need care to be taken by ordinary citizens, as well as by the »professional water suppliers«. It is not just the local authorities and the state that will be responsible, but everybody. This will also not be simple, even if it is possible to imagine fluent transitions from volunteer to paid work.

Ordinary citizens are only likely to take responsibility for water, and higher charges for developing a sustainable water culture will only be accepted, if people are aware of the value of water. One, perhaps even the most important, way of conveying this value is the natural and designed aesthetic of water. Pleasure in water conveyed by the senses and reflection about the condition of water stimulated by the senses are paths to sustainability.

Fortunately this is not all just a pipe-dream or a piece of woolly-headed idealism, but a great deal of it has already been set in motion, and a lot of people are working on keeping it in motion. Of course this is not a simple path, and there are many questions to be answered: can we afford ecology? Are ecology and urban life contradictions in terms? Do town-dwellers want to address, or better, under what conditions can they address, ecological urban redevelopment? How can ecology become a guideline for future cities? What do ecological aesthetics mean in concrete terms? Finally all these questions boil down to one key question: how can ecology be fixed in town-dwellers' minds as a meaningful project?

The town of Hannoversch Münden is addressing these questions with the »Wasserspuren« (Water-Traces) project. Three central squares around the church and the town hall are to be designed in such a way that the qualities of water can be experienced visually and acoustically. The town is between the rivers Fulda and Werra, and its history has been affected both for good and ill by these rivers. It is creating a new interpretation of its relationship with water as part of the natural environment. Traditionally urban squares, as something shaped and designed by man, are set against the ultimately uncontrolled nature of rivers. Now they are to convey the ecology of the whole habitat, of the city and of nature, to the townspeople.

New planning approaches have to be taken if a project of this kind is to succeed. The less conventional and tried-and-tested the aims of a piece of planning are, the earlier the well-trodden paths of planning have to be abandoned. Planners and architects, artists and townspeople start to co-operate on developing and implementing the project. Planners, artists and townspeople developed planning suggestions in joint workshops, under an outside chairman who was familiar with the town and its characteristics. These ideas were then put to a jury of external experts and local politicians. This was intended to produce high-quality designs and also to develop co-operation between the planners and artists involved. In this way the initiators of the process hoped that the townspeople would not just be involved in developing concepts and plans, but they would be protagonists in their own right, and thus also disseminators of the planning idea. Politics and administration create the general conditions needed for this process.

We call this kind of planning »deep participation«. But it does not just go beyond the boundary between citizen and planning, but also beyond the boundary between the various views taken by the involved. Artists, landscape designers, architects and townspeople work in a team, without changing or confusing their roles. Administration and politics admit an open process, with results that are often surprising. The political culture also benefits from the fact that politicians and administrators prove they are open to discussion.

The townspeople were informed – at first via the local press, then at meetings intended to provide information – about the new design and the possibility of being actively involved in the process themselves. Shortly before the protagonists' first plenary meeting a good third of all the people of Hannoversch Münden knew about the new project they were about to be involved in. Private individuals working with artists and planners in so-called planning workshops were the key point of the active participation. These workshops were intended to come up with a joint design concept. The suggestions were examined and reported on by a jury of outside planners and local politicians or members of the administration, and then »returned« to the planners and artists for revision, with suggestions and corrections. The participating townspeople could also familiarize themselves with other groups' ideas during the workshops. If a process like this is successful, the townspeople who are actively involved can also help to disseminate the ideas that the other planning teams come up with.

But the innovative potential is essentially to be found in the constellation of townspeople-planners-artists as an active group. A constellation of this kind, with the minimum involvement possible by politicians, administrators and the other usual interested parties, really is new. At the design phase in particular it is relieved of pressure from the particular interests that usually impinge upon planning processes.

By the time EXPO 2000 opened, the town's newly designed squares were ready to be assessed by the townspeople and visitors. We asked a representative cross-section of townspeople for their opinion of the new design.

In reply to the question »What do you think about each of the squares?«, in the case of Kirchplatz 60.9% said »pleasant«, 21.1% »unpleasant« and 18% were indifferent. The equivalent figures from the poll in September 1997 were 54.6%, 10.6% and 26.8%. In the case of the intermediate square, 56.6% of respondents were positive about the design, 21.5% negative and 21.9% indifferent. Three years before the same question had produced proportions of 15.8%, 39.5% and 44.7% respectively. And finally for Rathausplatz, in 2000 65.3% of respondents reacted positively, 19.9% negatively and 14.7% indifferently. In 1997 the equivalent figures were 70.9%, 8.2% and 20.9%.

If we compare the surveys taken in 1997, when the squares were in their original condition, it is clear how much the townspeople's opinion differs. In the case of Rathausplatz, which in 1997 was in a condition acceptable to the townspeople, the renewal of the pavement, shifting the market to this square and including it in the »Wasserspuren« project met with a positive response from most people, but this group has become smaller. There are now also more people who find the reconstructed square unpleasant. In the case of Kirchplatz, which has been clearly redesigned and makes an unambiguous reference to the theme of »Wasserspuren«, there is more general approval. The highest level of acceptance is found in the intermediate square that has changed from being a municipal bus-stop to an aquatic urban space.

Two things are clear here. There is not a great deal of additional gain to be had from a base where acceptance levels are already high. On the contrary, supporters of the old conditions turn against the »new« design in greater numbers. Secondly the key thematic design, in this case the idea of »Wasserspuren«, seems to have been convincing. And this increases in proportion with the unpopularity of the square in its old state.

Ecological aesthetics are not always successful even when townspeople are profoundly involved in the planning process. But firm commitment to the theme is probably the way to broaden identification to the greatest possible extent.

# »Water-traces« in Hannoversch Münden

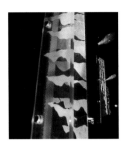

The carefully devised lighting design means that viewers can always find new perspectives in the water.

Three ramps between the fields reveal the rhythmic flow patterns on the surface of the water.

People wonder about the source of major rivers from time to time. And there are some that do not have a source at all. The Weser, for example. It seems that it got its name because people could not agree whether the river should be called the Fulda or the Werra from the point at which they meet in Hannoversch Münden. This town, now called Hann. Münden for short, is near Kassel, and – as is the case with many places on rivers – water is very important, bringing great happiness and great misery. And yet the two rivers that meet here flow past behind the old town, and are quite insignificant for it and in the awareness of many people.

A well as three rivers, the town also has three connected squares in the heart of the old quarter: Kirchplatz, the square between the church and the town hall and the market-place. When decisions were made about traffic-calming, people had the idea of redesigning and revitalizing the squares. A theme was quickly found: »water-traces« – the paths followed by watercourses – were to be made visible. Registering as an associate Expo location provided an immovable completion deadline.

The way in which project was organized made a major contribution to its success. Five working groups made up of residents, landscape architects and fine artists, chaired by an architect, developed a wide range of ideas. Experts worked together and with laymen in an open atmosphere and finally created six works of art in the ensemble of squares, which slopes downwards from south to north.

The Dreiseitl studio built its contribution to this system, which is fed mainly by rainwater, in the square between the church and the town hall. There are four terraced steps here, like a large folded carpet. The water bubbles out of the topmost, narrowest terrace, and runs over the next three, each of which drops through a small height.

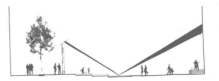

The rhythmic patterns on the surface of the water are reflected on to the large town hall façade by cleverly devised lighting management.

A narrow stainless steel gutter accepts the water at the bottom and takes it back to the circulation tank. And now people of all ages can go in search of the traces left by the water on this carpet. One aspect is that the water leaves all sorts of different traces because of differences in the subsoil. But then people can leave their own traces or tracks here – which was very important to the artists and planners. The nature of the flow is changed if people simply step into the pool. But you can also change the flow pattern by using the plates, slides and wave-making devices that are placed around the carpet.

Experience, touch and just get going and play without worrying

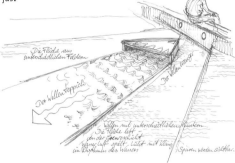

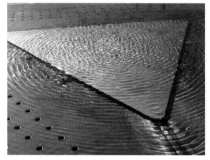

The shallow water allows for playing on the water »carpet«. Three steles with light and sounds accentuate the square.

The overall effect is further enhanced by three steles: V-shaped glass about five metres high sits on a steel plinth and is lit obliquely after dark. Light is then caught by a sand-blasted relief, and produces an image. Light then shoots in its turn through the gap in the V to the mirror at the top, which casts the beam on to the pool of water whose mobile structure is then reflected on to the wall of the town hall. Loudspeakers mounted in the steles throw artistically alienated voices or sounds made by water out into the scene, as a pattern of urban noise. Here water is clearly making a material effect. Flow images trigger ideas, projections give rise to associations, water leaves traces.

# Interior courtyard of an old people's home in Stuttgart

Water glides softly through stone channels, makes a pleasing sound in little waterfalls then disappears again among the aquatic plants. The sound brings a sense of magic to the space, and life into the old people's home.

It is not just young people who like to have greenery around them, and who look for ways of getting closer to nature. This need does not diminish in old age, but old people cannot always do anything about it entirely on their own. And so internal spaces with a lot of plants in them in places where old people are confined and can only control how they spend their own time to a limited extent are all the more important: in locations like old people's homes and nursing-homes. Old people in the Nicolas-Cusanus-Haus in Stuttgart have an enormous range of plants available to them all the year round, set in a landscape with water running through it.

The first impression is often of being in the tropical house in a botanical garden, though without the warm and humid greenhouse atmosphere that quickly drives Western Europeans back out into the fresh air. This idea comes from a luxuriant display of mainly evergreen plants, in a glazed inner courtyard covering eight hundred square metres. The old people knew many of these plants on a smaller scale from their own window-sills at home, discovered them in their original form on journeys to faraway countries or have seen them in zoos or botanical gardens. In their new home, which could be their last one, they find banana and palm trees, rubber plants and ferns arranged so as to focus all the memories and experiences associated with them. Most of them were provided by the botanical gardens in Heidelberg.

But the atmosphere that has been created would not have been possible without water as an element. It is often first noticed on a different level of perception, because sometimes it can only be heard and not seen. But the residents are particularly fond of these sounds. The constant splashing and glugging creates a comfortable, indeed luxurious acoustic background, masking distant scraps of conversation and keeping

The centre of the building is a green oasis at all times of the year.

The courtyard offers
changing perspectives.

people's own intimate conversations private. And it also suggests taking a closer look. Water makes its effect here above all because of the surfaces it runs down, from which it drips and over which it runs away. All these features are made of stone, and discreetly sculpted. For example, long horizontal scales are worked into steeply sloping lumps of stone, and the water drips down these, leaving some parts dry and allowing different kinds of moss to develop. Natural stone blocks that were excavated in the course of building were piled up, and Herbert Dreiseitl had meandering and branching grooves chiselled and cut into them, and the water flows through as though it had made these pathways for itself. On the ground floor level the water finally ends up in troughs and basins after running under little bridges and washing around stepping stones. The inner courtyard of the Nicolaus-Cusanus-Haus has set new standards for old people's living conditions, indeed for humane living conditions. The residents enjoy expansive views of terraces, steps and paths on four storeys, or can sit in sheltered alcoves away from it all. They feel at home in temperatures between 18 and 25 degrees – and also that they are being cared for in a very special way.

The combination of water,
natural stone and vegetation conveys a sense of life,
and creates new moods
at various times of day.

The natural stones have
been treated artistically,
the gliding wave structures
swirl like pennants.

General plan of the inner
courtyard with designs
for water and vegetation

# Schafbrühl housing estate, Tübingen

By making models together children and adults develop a high level of acceptance and care in dealing with the water features that are subsequently installed.

Retaining and releasing water – weirs give children a lot of things to play with.

The sixties and seventies left behind a number of dormitory estates with no sense of human scale, unstructured commercial areas and access roads that take up far too much space. Agricultural land on urban peripheries was turned into building land in order to create space of affordable housing. But the quality was generally low. This also applied to Tübingen, the medieval town on the Neckar.

In the mid eighties, when ecological and social components were becoming more important as factors in urban development, an insurance company decided to build the Schafbrühl housing complex on the edge of the »Waldhäuser Ost« hilltop estate. Shortly after completion this project by architects Eble & Sambeth, Oed, Häfele became the model estate in South Germany for sustainable building practice.

Surrounded as they were by high-rise buildings, commercial premises and a sports centre, the planners had only one choice: they had to put a great deal of thought into creating an inner life for the estate. The traffic free inner courtyards were planned by landscape architect Christoph Harms, and Herbert Dreiseitl was responsible for open integration of rainwater. Water in a whole series of manifestations attracts adults and children alike here – from outside the neighbourhood as well. It flows via rills into a fishpond or finds its way via a brook containing stone blocks and in which weirs control the speed of flow. A cistern collects surplus water and from here it is pumped back into the cycle, which also includes a water playground.

The Virbella installation attracts attention as a design – but as a sculpture it also makes other effects. Water flows through organically shaped concrete dishes, thus creating currents and counter-currents that stimulate children to play in it. The turbulence dishes also reduce the negative diffusion levels in the water created by the pump and the

pressure pipe. This is important in its turn for the survival of the pond-life.

At the opening day, visitors met for a Water Day workshop. By drawing, making models and building rills they got to know the central element in their courtyard – which has meant that since 1986 they have pretty well been able to forget the inhospitable surroundings of their estate.

Water runs through the estate's inner courtyards, offering children a safe place to play.

A simple drain can show an interesting phenomenon: the formation of an eddy

Site plan: The water arteries
run through the inner
courtyard areas.

# A fountain for the blind in Ulm

The Blind Fountain with its little square framed by the green spaces of the 1980 Baden-Württemberg Horticultural Show

When we hear a beeping sound at traffic-light controlled pedestrian crossings we are reminded: there are people who can't see. The number of sensual experiences that they miss seems infinite. But this is a mistaken impression, caused by lack of understanding for the more sophisticated way in which this social minority perceives things. It is only when we come to think maturely about what people who can't see want and are able to do, when possibilities for our blind fellow human beings are included in the planning process, that space can be created for blind people.

Horticultural shows offer outstanding opportunities for experiments with urban open space. The city of Ulm acknowledged this when it was setting up the first Baden-Württemberg Horticultural Show and commissioned the Leonberg landscape architects Eppinger & Schmid to create a fragrance and tactility garden there. The fountain planned by Herbert Dreiseitl for this garden was considered to be a particularly attractive feature, and this is still the case, even though the garden is somewhat hidden away. Dreiseitl designed the Blind Fountain, christened after a workshop at the adult education centre, in co-operation with blind people. It was only in the course of making models of three-dimensional bodies with them, and by listening to their experience and discussing their ideas that he was able to decide on materials, shapes and a structure for the future users. Polished, organically shaped dishes are placed on a stepped concrete plinth. These are the so-called flowforms devised by the British artist John Wilkes after intensive experimentation with flow patterns. The water emerges at a height of about a metre, then flows through the basins in three directions, creating audible currents and countercurrents, before reaching the step below, and then eventually ground level. The sound means that the blind visitors can

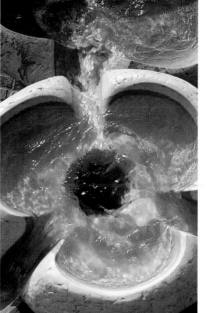

always orientate themselves, and thus feel secure.

From the fountain the water flows through a gap in the main path to a wet biotope. This watercourse subtly links the stone fountain to the spawning waters of dragonflies and water beetles, making it an integral part of the garden as a whole. A small proportion of fresh water maintains the required water quality at all times.

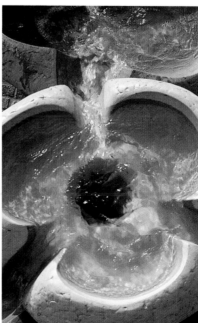

A fountain to be understood – conceived as a tactile field for blind people to experience

Pulsating veils of water form a membrane that emits a rhythmic sound.

From the source basin the water is distributed into the other swinging dishes.

The Blind Fountain as a peaceful place to relax among the gentle sounds of water

Top view of the feature showing the arrangement of the individual swinging dishes

# Water playground in Pforzheim

Children like asking questions, and sometimes they ask a lot. Adults don't always like explaining things, rarely do it vividly and sometimes not at all – if they don't know the answer. This is why children's playgrounds exist. They can look for things to do there, set themselves problems and work out how to solve them. Water is always on the move, creates a path for itself, comes to the surface, collects, seeps away – and raises questions. How does water come to the surface, why does it flow in the way it does, where do I stand in the cycle of coming to the surface and running away?

A water playground in the South German town of Pforzheim tries to provide answers to these many questions. It stands on the northern edge of the Black Forest, and in 1992 staged the regional horticultural show, using a very varied landscape featuring all aspects of water in an area of four thousand square metres. »Learning through play«, an appeal from progressive educationalists, is something that is done here by children and a large number of adults as well. And in two contrasting spheres: nature and civilization.

In the natural section the water appears in gently modelled brooks flowing through meadows and irrigation areas. The water rises from various clefts in a round stone basin or emerges as a surface spring from the luxuriant growth around basins on the site, then flows on its way, by now a little brook, to the civilization section. There it splashes, twists and winds through everything relating to water technology's evolution history. Ancient devices for raising water (the Egyptian shadoof), Archimedean screws, a medieval well-shaft and a rotary pump are arranged together in a chain of play-stations. Visitors can and should play in both zones, but while tranquillity is the key feature of the natural area, fun and games are the order of the day in the civilized zone.

Herbert Dreiseitl had the water-raising devices arranged in such a way that it is almost impossible to resist a water-drawing competition. For example, of the four Archimedean screws, two are placed at the top and two at the bottom, so that two teams of two can play at raising water on to the higher level. In this upper channel, into which the other raising devices also drain, the water continues on its way to a play castle. Here water comes to the surface again, and flows away in various directions when retention weirs are opened and closed, to an experiment channel or an aqueduct. All these play-stations have turned out to need little maintenance over the years.

The water playground is in precisely the right place between the little river Enz and the historic waterworks. A proportion of about 20 % of fresh water is introduced into the cycle from the waterworks, to meet the purity requirements. The playground is near the city centre, and has drawn visitors in large numbers ever since it opened. This is probably due to the generous provision of busy and quiet areas and its unique character, which is also expressed in all the play-stations, each of which is unique in its own right. Here asking questions can turn into a game.

The ancient devices for raising water, Archimedean screws and the shadoof in the background teach history through the medium of play.

A water playground by the river – here everyone can join in. Water can be raised, played with, and experienced.

The lockkeeper at the moated castle gives permission to proceed – a water-channel with mobile obstacles, research into water behaviour in the playground

The medieval well-shaft, discovered by children working as a team

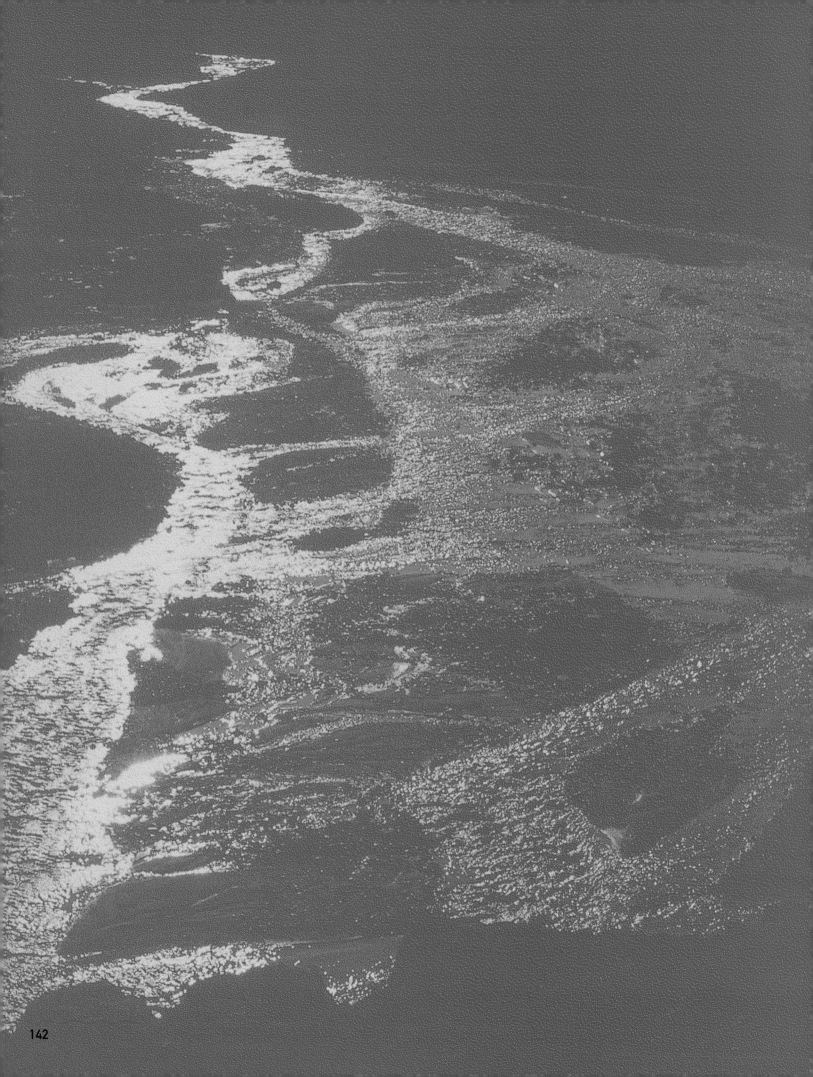

# From the idea to the finished object

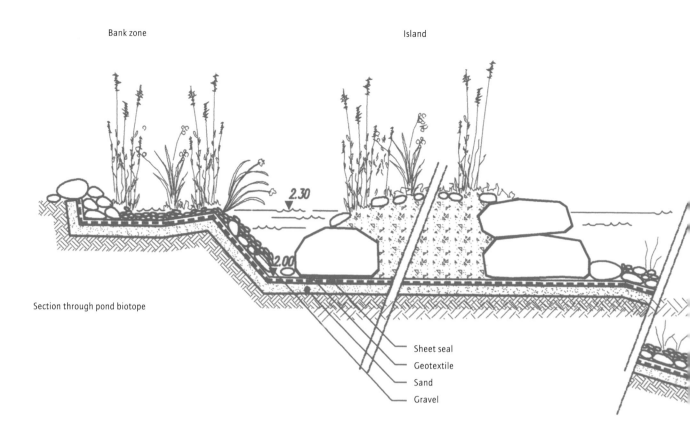

Bank zone         Island

2.30

2.00

Section through pond biotope

Sheet seal
Geotextile
Sand
Gravel

**Water can be a problem in urban open spaces. Building water features seems prohibitively expensive, too many things can go wrong, and maintenance is too expensive. But when the water quality is right, pumps, filters and control devices are working properly, the parts of the building that come in contact with the water are not damaged and when water, along with light and sound effects, turns boring places into exciting ones, no one wants to be without it. But however easily and light-heartedly water flows and splashes – it needs expert handling in urban landscapes.**

Constructed water features are always individual objects. They emerge from interplay between the possibilities offered by the site and clients' and planners' ideas and wishes. The techniques used to install and run them are as varied as the water features themselves. They are rarely to be had off the peg, but need a technical concept that is individually tailored to their location.

But on the other hand there are always standards and guidelines to be taken into account, for example those applying to the depth of the water or water hygiene. There are a wide range of regulations applying to these in different countries. Experience shows that these can be interpreted individually in terms of each particular situation. This is especially true if new and unconventional ideas are being realized: it is innovative concepts above all that mean thinking beyond existing norms. Here the key recommendation is that the responsible

authorities should be involved in the search for new solutions from the outset.

The following brings together a few hints on building and running water features that have emerged over the years from day-to-day work in the studio.

### Sourcing and water quality

A fundamental criterion for the building and running of water features is the quality of the water. This is affected by physical, chemical and biological processes in the water itself and by its interplay with its immediate surroundings.

**Water sourcing:** Water features usually tap into the local water supply which generally means using drinking water. It is also becoming increasingly attractive to think of using available surface run-off, drainage water or roof collected rainwater.

The origins and quality of water are crucial in terms of its possible use. When concerning a complex planning task, it is advisable to consult experts like limnologists to develop parameters for anticipated water quality. It is also important to identify questions about water hygiene and upkeep as quality requirements even during the design phase. Different standards apply according to the purpose for which the water is being used. The more the water comes into direct contact with people, for example with children playing, the more

Dieter Grau, Alexander Edel, Gerhard Hauber, Herbert Dreiseitl

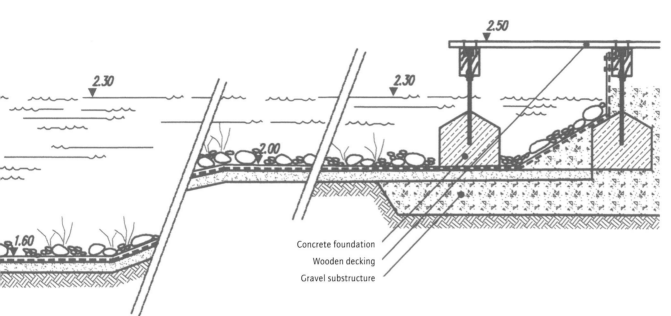

2.50

2.30　2.30

2.00

1.60

Concrete foundation
Wooden decking
Gravel substructure

drinking water or at least bathing water quality will be required. As a rule water features that suggest drinking, in other words raised features, should use drinking water, while bathing water quality is usually sufficient for features at ground level, or for pools.

The interplay between water and its built environment should be taken into account at the planning stage. Materials like concrete or mortar can have a significant effect on water chemistry, increasing the calcium content and raising the pH value of the water drastically. This can have a very negative effect on flora and fauna and in extreme cases damage the surface of materials.

Certain nutrients and germs will get into the water naturally by rainfall and can cause biological surface growth like algae or bacteria. The aim should be to keep this within tolerable bounds. Unrealistic expectations on the part of the client, like clear water that is free of algae at all times, should thus be discussed in advance. Such a requirement makes enormous technical demands that can only be met by using chemicals, UV filtration and other elaborate techniques. Using chemicals to purify water often turns out to be a dead end – it is expensive in the long run and ecologically dubious for the water. It can also create a number of peripheral problems, such as restricted plant growth or offensive odours.

Water is much more readily accepted when it is clear. For this reason attention should be paid from the outset to the rubbish and pollutants that will come into contact with the water and to their sources. Some things will fall into the water naturally, some as a result of human intervention. Fallen

leaves or road dust, but also food for ducks and fish (this should not be underestimated as a problem), and remains of human food and packaging will likely end up in the water. Any open water is polluted by such materials, which are either dissolved in it, or remain undissolved. It is therefore very important to know about any sources of pollution at the planning stage, and to estimate the nature and scale of their possible effects on the water feature.

The choice of which water technology is ultimately installed is influenced by all these prior considerations and investigations of processes in the water system. Courageous decisions about ecologically sensible solutions take pressure off the environment and can set new standards that lead to genuine innovation. Learning from nature and using the insights gained for new concepts is also a relevant planning approach here.

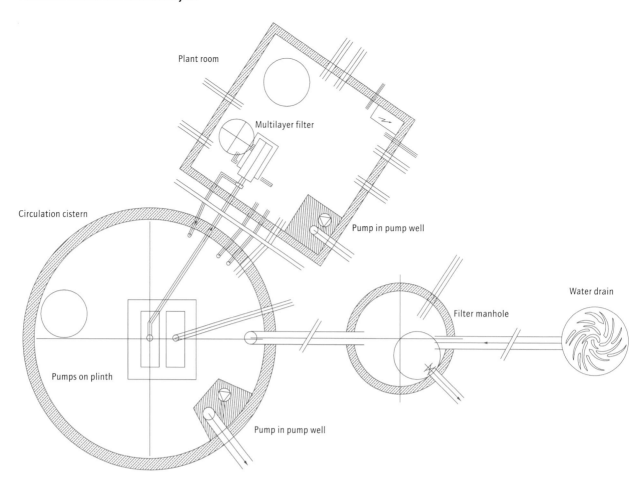

General plan for
plant room and
circulation cistern

Plant room

Multilayer filter

Circulation cistern

Pump in pump well

Water drain

Filter manhole

Pumps on plinth

Pump in pump well

### Construction elements

Water features cannot be built without technical equipment like reservoirs, pumps, filters and control devices. These are needed to purify the water, to store it and to control its circulation.

**Storage and circulation cisterns:** All water features with a circulating water system need a cistern or storage reservoir to ensure that there is always enough water available for them to run on. When small quantities of water are involved it is usually sufficient to install a cistern near the feature where the water can fall to by gravity. The cistern or reservoir has to be big enough for all the water to be stored after the feature has been switched off. The circulating volume consists of the amount of water circulating in all the pipes, channels and pools, and has to be specifically fixed for each feature.

It is not unusual for mistakes to be made when calculating for large volumes of water. The volume flowing out of a feature must be the same as the volume flowing in. The smaller and narrower the outlet, the more the water will back up. This variation in water level has thus to be assessed as a volume and the water level has to be able to rise accordingly.

Water from the cistern is either brought by suction to the pumps in the plant room or pumped directly back into the circulation system by a submerged pump in the cistern. When features have a low-lying body of water like a pool or pond, these can be used as a reservoir and thus a separate cistern is not needed. Additional water is then fed directly into the body

of water. It is important that every storage reservoir or cistern is provided with an overflow as well as a drainage outlet so that it can be emptied and cleaned at regular intervals.

**Pumps:** It is seldom that a water feature can be set to run on a natural slope. Normally the water has to be circulated artificially with pumps. As a rule these are modern rotary pumps that are set up in either a wet or a dry state. Dirty-water pumps are recommended if high dirt levels are anticipated.

Our experience is that it makes sense to run small fountains and watercourses with a circulation volume of up to 300 l/min with submerged pumps. But not all makes are entirely suitable for this. Submerged pumps are usually more reasonably priced than dry-installed pumps, as they do not need their own control room and can be placed directly in the reservoir. They are more expensive to maintain than dry-installed pumps. Submerged pumps must always be set up so that they are sufficiently above the bottom of the feature to avoid clogging with mud.

Dry-installed pumps are recommended when several pumps are required or they have to be set up in sequence. They are more accessible and thus easier to maintain, but they need adequate installation space. The best place is in a building near to the water feature or a readily accessible service shaft. Here it is essential to build in a bottom outlet to the channel and also ventilation where necessary. Dry-installed pumps do not run silently even when fitted with vibration dampers; for this reason they should be sited so that sound

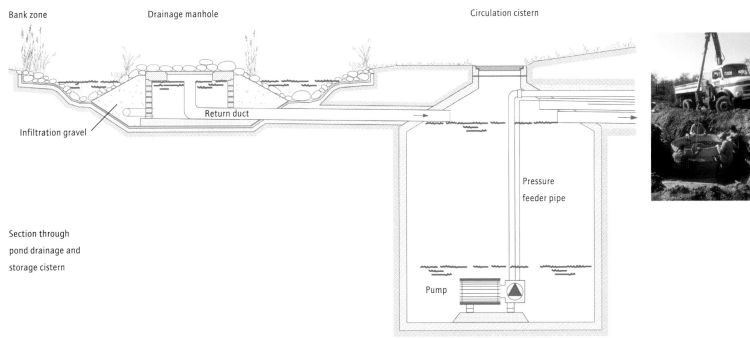

Bank zone    Drainage manhole    Circulation cistern

Return duct

Infiltration gravel

Pressure
feeder pipe

Section through
pond drainage and
storage cistern

Pump

emissions are kept reduced to a minimum.

The size of the pumps should not be decided until the volume of circulating water has been fixed. The manufacturer's technical specifications can be used as a guide. In the case of prototype features with special flow effects the size of the pumps should not be fixed without testing in a full-scale model. A certain circulation reserve should always be built in when choosing the size of the pumps so that the water quantities can be regulated if necessary. Maximum performance in relation to energy used can be achieved by pumps with automatic revolution speed controls, but this elaborate technology does not come cheap.

**Filters:** In nature water is continuously filtered in a number of ways such as percolating through vegetated soil, or by water animals. Filtering of this kind is also needed in artificial waters, especially when a lot of foreign bodies may find their way into it. Man contributes to this as well as nature – for example with plastic bags, cola cans, food scraps, plastic straws, cigarette ends and so on.

The first planning aim should always be to avoid dirt and rubbish entering the water in the first place. Where this is not possible the substances, which are often floating and do not dissolve, must be filtered out as soon after they enter the water as possible. In the case of circulation features this is done by coarse pre-filters like skimmers, rakes of perforated metal sheeting that are usually built into the feedback to the cistern. Various grades, from coarse to fine filtering, should be chosen, according to the amount of dirt involved. A filter with a mesh larger than 10 mm is considered coarse in this context. These should be simple and quick to handle, as otherwise manual cleaning tends to be carried out rarely or not at all. Stainless steel has proved its worth as a construction material for these pre-filters.

It makes sense to use automatic filter systems as well as pre-filters in more complex features; as a rule they are installed on the delivery side of the pump. These filters, including fast sand filters and micro-sieves, are outstandingly well suited for removing fine particles like weeds or floating matter from the circulating water. Maintenance requirements are low, as these filters can be set to clean themselves automatically from time to time. Automatic filters should be fitted in the bypass

Section through
equipment room

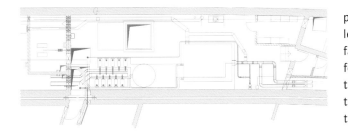

Operational diagram
for circulation technology

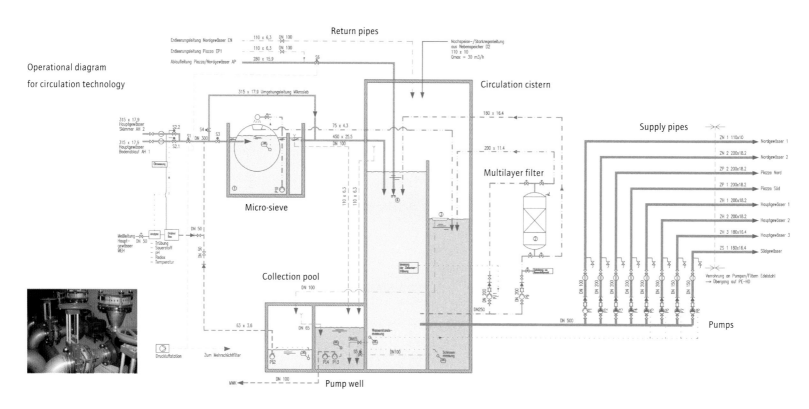

to the circulation tank, and should ideally be able to filter about 50 % of the total water in circulation.

We have found that naturally developed sand or bottom filters, here called purification biotopes, are suitable for many water features. They are particularly appropriate for features and systems that allow the watercourse to develop naturally to a certain extent, and that have sufficient space available. They have various advantages; they form second-hand biotopes, do not need any additional energy and are not expensive to maintain. As with any other planting, dead vegetable matter and foreign bodies have to be removed from time to time. The winter months are most suitable for this.

**Regulation and monitoring:** Every water system needs regulation. This ensures that the various input points are provided with the appropriate quantities of water at the required time. When the water level drops in the cistern or the body of water an electrical or mechanical sensor should monitor the water level and ensure that the necessary extra water is fed in. The control boxes and all the meters should always be installed above maximum water level in a separate shaft or in the cellars of an adjacent building. In the case of larger and more complex features there will be meters for certain parameters like pH value, temperature, oxygen content or nutrient levels in the water, working continuously or sporadically. These values then form a basis for precise analysis of the water. Some clients like the feature to be monitored so that they can optimize development and also the maintenance of the system and the related costs on the basis of suggestions from experts.

Section through
purification biotope

Purification biotope

Bank zone

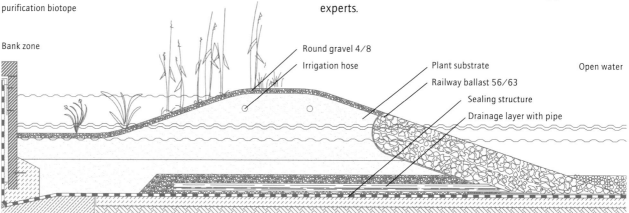

Round gravel 4/8
Irrigation hose
Plant substrate
Railway ballast 56/63
Sealing structure
Drainage layer with pipe
Open water

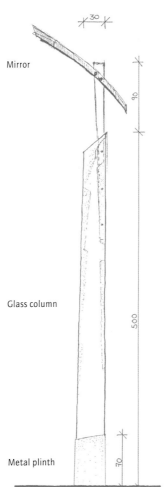

30

Mirror

90

Sound and light
column

Glass column

500

Metal plinth

70

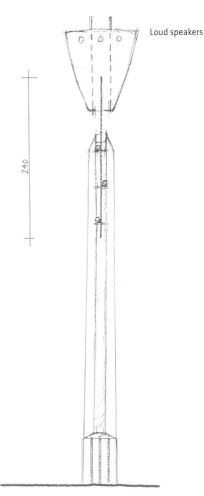

Loud speakers

240

**Light/sound technology:** Lighting and sound effects are becoming increasingly desired by the client. They enhance the effects of a water feature and give the experience a new dimension, especially in the evening and at night. It is essential to investigate the existing light and sound situation of the site, in order to assess their influence.

In many cases no elaborate electronic systems are needed. The interaction of air and water alone produces all sorts of sound patterns that can be used to good effect within a spatial concept. The rush of water has other qualities to offer than traffic noise, for example, and can be used deliberately to dampen or mask unpleasant noises and at the same time offers the opportunity to create a special atmosphere in a particular place.

Water cannot be lit like other objects. If artificial light is used, care has to be taken that the water itself can direct the light, and here reflected light is crucial. Before choosing a light source it is essential to conduct experiments to establish the desired effect of light on the water.

This effect is crucially dependent on the reflection of light from the surface of the water: it is only this that makes the water visible. Skilful light installation can also achieve these effects in twilight and at night.

If lighting is to be effective it is essential that the source points are positioned correctly. Lighting the water directly is not recommended, as the light would be reflected only at certain points. It is better to draw the observer's attention to adjacent objects. They will be reflected from the surface and will produce the fluctuating images associated with water

with even a very little movement.

Lighting devices should be chosen in such a way that insects are not attracted in greater numbers, and to avoid increased weed growth in the water. This means that halogen lamps with a large UV output are not suitable; metal vapour lamps tend to be most used today.

Fibre-optic technology is particularly suitable for underwater lighting. The key feature here is that the light source can be placed at a safe distance from the body of water, and the fibre technology can take the light wherever it is wanted.

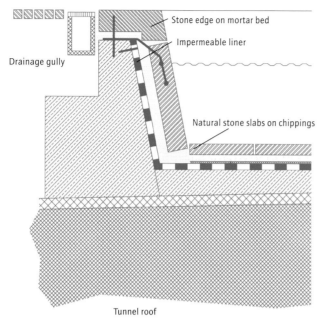

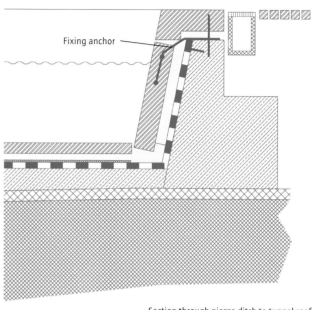

Drainage gully

Stone edge on mortar bed

Impermeable liner

Natural stone slabs on chippings

Fixing anchor

Tunnel roof

Section through piazza ditch to tunnel roof

### Construction technology

Technical aspects of construction are of crucial importance for interesting water features with high design values. Interest is focused on the following four areas: sealing, foundations, materials and connections.

**Sealing:** Natural seals like clay can rarely be used in built water features. There are many sealing processes that are quite close to nature, but a certain diffusion loss has to be anticipated with all of them. Such processes are suitable only when continuous supply and constant water level are guaranteed.

When choosing a sealant the necessities arising from the specific situation have to be set off against the technical and financial input involved. The following criteria should be considered: the qualities of the building land, the geometry and surface of the feature, the desired water quality, the planned building phases and the cost.

Water features that are supplied and drained naturally make fewer demands in terms of sealing than those that rely on an artificial supply of drinking water or rainwater. However, minimal water loss should be a prime consideration even for small water features, for ecological and financial reasons.

Plastic sheeting is very adaptable as a sealing material, and is well suited to features with complex contours and very diverse geometry. But natural forms can be constructed with it as well. Many water features have to take differing settling rates into account. Flexible sheeting is suitable here, as it is relatively easy to install on the spot, almost regardless of the weather. A whole variety of materials are available; of course their environmental friendliness must be given higher priority than technical suitability and economic viability.

If the substructure is something stable like concrete, for instance, a non-shrink grouting compound can also be used as a seal. It bonds firmly with the base and is simple to apply even if the geometry is complex. Coverings like natural stone slabs can be fitted directly to the rigid seal. This is also appropriate for fixed materials like concrete and steel, but does not work with flexible connections or expansion joints; other sealing processes have to be used here.

Water features in the shape of simple and rigid structures can be built in non-permeable concrete. However, these are appropriate only when the subsoil is stable, certain dimensions are not exceeded and walls of an adequate thickness can be built. The statics of water-proof concrete make it particularly suitable as a base for large prefabricated sections.

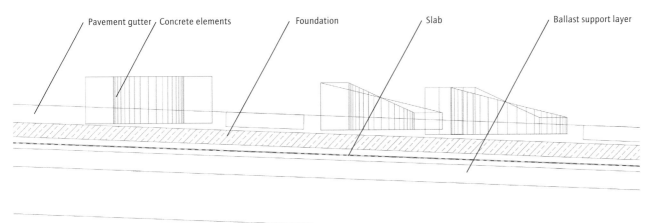

Pavement gutter / Concrete elements  Foundation  Slab  Ballast support layer

Section through watercourse

**Foundations:** Semi-natural lakes and ponds do not need rigid foundations. But fountains, pools and other built water features are particularly sensitive to subsoil settling, which can lead to cracks and leaks. What is usually needed here is foundations that can have a frost-free base and that are designed to meet the structural loading. The dimensions and thickness of the foundations are based on the weight, geometry, size and tolerance limit of the surface building.

**Choice of materials:** Unlike other structures, built water-features have surfaces that are always wet. For this reason it is important to use materials that are structurally stable and also frostproof in colder regions. Another important factor is that chemical and physical reactions of materials can be different and more aggressive in contact with water than in air, and vary with the characteristics of the water (pH value, temperature etc.). Building materials must be chosen to withstand such processes in the long term. Water quality must also be taken into account when choosing materials, as substances dissolved out of mortar or concrete can have a lasting deleterious effect on water chemistry.

In the case of earth and mineral substrates, chemical stability and the purity of the material are important factors. Organic components should be avoided wherever possible, as they raise nutrient levels and thus promote the growth of algae.

The colour of these materials is a key influence on the visual impact of the water; here dark shades are generally better for reflections on the surface of the water whereas-

lighter shades are suitable for showing reflections on the bottom. However, it is not so important to design the surface of these coverings elaborately, as the effect they make will be considerably reduced by the natural surface growth that occurs in any water. This growth can only be avoided by mechanical cleaning or the use of chemicals.

Water features in which people are intended to walk should have non-slip surfaces to minimize the risk of falling. Sharp-edged installations should also be avoided as they increase the risk of injury.

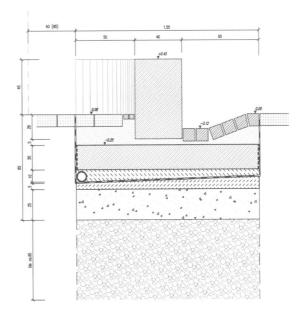

Section through concrete element run and water-course

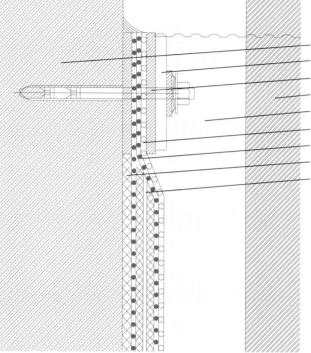

Concrete support structure
Fan jet 6/60
Neoprene
Water borderstone
Mortar filling 45 mm
Protective layer 3 mm
Waterproof layer 2,5 mm
Fleece 500 g/m2
Control sensor

Fitting the waterproof
layer with adhesive strip

**Interfaces:** Natural watercourses are always in a state of dynamic interchange with their surroundings, losing water through outflow, evaporation and infiltration. Artificial water features would quickly lose their water to the surrounding area. To prevent this, the interface is particularly important, as well as sealing.

The interface between inflow, outflow, pipes and walls always presents a potential danger in terms of leaks; this is where most problems occur in practice. Different construction methods are required according to the nature of the seal. Connections through sheeting require fundamentally different flange constructions from those used for pierced concrete, for instance. For this reason precise and early planning is needed here, and particularly careful attention must always be paid to the construction and detailing of these points. Some specialist manufacturers offer prefabricated pipe ducting for seals of all kinds.

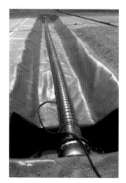

Detail of pipework

Seal insert for water
under pressure
Filter pipe DN 150/DN 300

Sliding bearing/foil
Granular subbase B 10
Sand bed for pipeline

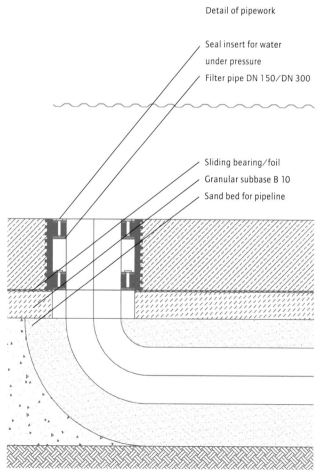

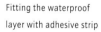

Construction option 1   Construction option 2       Construction option 3       Waterproof bottom

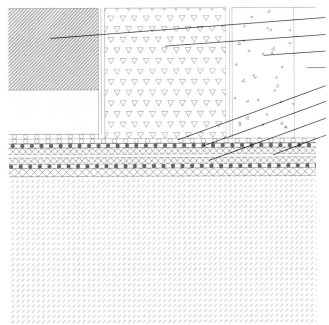

Natural granite slab
Railway ballast
Gravel 5/25
Substrate
Protective layer 3 mm
Waterproof layer 2,5 mm
Fleece 500 g/m2
Control sensor

## Running and maintenance

People who own and run a water feature will soon become disillusioned with it if it costs more than a modest amount to maintain. Planning should thus aim to avoid high maintenance and running expenses. A number of very creatively successful water features have been closed because of technical problems, the need for frequent repair work and unduly high running costs.

Traditionally fountains and other running water features are closed in winter. But it is possible to run them all the year round if appropriate preventive measures are taken, like frostproof water storage facilities and a heated water supply.

A thorough planning approach will pay particular attention to the later running of the water feature. More or less elaborate solutions will be selected according to location. The centre of a large city imposes different requirements and thus needs different creative and technical concepts from those appropriate to small towns or villages. An intensively used feature should therefore not just be well designed, but above all well looked after as well. Here we must not fail to recognize that ornately designed components will always be more likely to be damaged than robust elements. The finished product should be selected to match the location in a way that does not encourage increasing tendencies to vandalism.

In the long run, water features work best if they are as clearly and simply planned as possible. Logical arrangements and structures for the various units and sections make them easier to service. To avoid periods of malfunction, or to keep them as short as possible, it makes sense for large water features to use parts from the same manufacturer. This makes it easy to replace components and also simplifies storage.

All electrical devices in the wet area inside and outside the water feature must be appropriately protected and fused to meet safety standards. This includes current failure protection circuits, damp and wet fittings, low voltage installations and appropriate earthing for all live electrical parts.

Staff often find a service manual helpful. This should contain lists of all the maintenance work needed, instructions on how to behave in case of emergency, and guidelines for running the system in winter.

# Technical data

**Page 14**

Town square
Hattersheim
**Client:**
Stadt Hattersheim
**Water design:**
Herbert Dreiseitl
**Landscape design:**
Atelier Dreiseitl
**Architect:**
Büro Walter,
Wiesbaden
**Stone masonry:**
Fa. Hettinger
**Planning and design:**
1988 – 1992
**Construction:**
1989 – 1993

Size: 4,600 m²
**Watercourse length:**
120 m
**Water surface:**
2,000 m² pond
**Total water volume:**
2,000 m³
**Flow rate:** 450 l/min
**Maximum water
depth:** 250 cm
**Minimum water
depth:** 5 cm
**Water treatment:**
Purification biotope
**Pump power:**
1.2 kW

**Page 20**

Musical fountain
L'Aubier near
Neuchâtel,
Switzerland
**Client:**
L'Aubier, Montezillon
**Design:**
Herbert Dreiseitl
**Details and
Landscape design:**
Atelier Dreiseitl
**Architect:**
Kurt Hofmann
**Metalworks:**
Metallatelier
David Fuchs
**Planning and design:**
1990
**Construction:**
1991 – 1992

Size:
Two storey object,
height 6 m
**System:**
Perforated collection
piping
**Length:** 30 m water-
course through the
building
**Flow rate:** 2 l/min
**Water treatment:**
Macro- and micro-
filtering systems

**Page 22**

Herne-Sodingen
Academy
**Client:**
EMC Entwicklungsge-
sellschaft Mont Cenis
**Water design:**
Atelier Dreiseitl
**Architects:**
Jourda Architects,
HHS Planer und
Architekten
**Project management:**
dmp GmbH
**Planning and design:**
1998 – 1999
**Construction:**
1999

**Watercourse length:**
180 m
**Water basin:** 720 m²
**Flow rate:**
250 l/min water-
course
3,200 l/min water
basin
**Water depth:** 30 cm
watercourse
40 cm water basin
**Cistern volume:**
10 m³ watercourse
12 m³ water basin
**Water treatment:**
Multi-layered filter
system
**Pump power:**
1.0 kW watercourse
3.0 kW water basin

**Page 28**

Watercourse and
water-wall
Gummersbach
**Client:**
Stadt Gummersbach
Sparkasse Gummers-
bach
**Water design:**
Herbert Dreiseitl
**Landscape design:**
Atelier Dreiseitl
**Urban design:**
Gruppe Hardtberg
**Architect:**
Axel von Reden
**Contractors:**
Glasgestaltung Dierig
Metallatelier Fuchs
**Planning and design:**
1997 – 1999
**Construction:**
1998 – 1999

**Length:** 200 m
**Circulation rate:**
500 l/min
**Water storage:** 30 m³
**Water treatment:**
Sand filter
**Pump power:** 2.5 kW

**Page 34**

Kogarah Town Square,
Sydney, Australia
**Client:**
Kogarah Council
**Water design:**
Herbert Dreiseitl
**Landscape design:**
Allen Jack & Cottier
(AJC)
**Architect:**
Allen Jack & Cottier
(AJC)
**Planning and design:**
1999 – 2000
**Construction:**
2000 – 2002

**Size:**
Town square 1,800 m²
**Watercourse length:**
40 m
**Cistern volume:**
100 m³ (watercourse,
toilets, carwash)
**Water treatment:**
Automatic sand filter

**Page 36**

Residential development »Im Park«, Bern-Ittigen, Switzerland
**Client:**
Berner Lebensversicherungs-Gesellschaft
**Water design:**
Herbert Dreiseitl
**Landscape design:**
Atelier Dreiseitl
**Architect:**
René Burkhalter AG, Architectur Design
**Planning and design:**
1988 – 1989
**Construction:**
1989 – 1990

**Size:** 6,000 m²
**Watercourse length:**
60 m
**Water surface:** 200 m²
**Total water volume:**
15 m³
**Flow rate:** 500 l/min
**Maximum water depth:** 40 cm
**Cistern volume:** 10 m³
**Water treatment:**
Technical filter
**Pump power:** 4 kW
**Total area:**
800 m² roof
**Residents:** 700
**Impermeable surface:**
60 %
**Annual rainfall:**
900 mm
**Drainage method:**
Open surface drains, retention pond

**Page 44**

Potsdamer Platz, Berlin
**Client:**
Stadt Berlin/
Debis Immobilien
**Water design:**
Atelier Dreiseitl
**Architects:**
Renzo Piano,
Christoph Kohlbecker
**Project management:**
Atelier Dreiseitl +
Peter Hausdorf
**Planning and design:**
1994 – 1998
**Construction:**
1997 – 1998

**Water surface:**
ca 12,000 m²
**Shoreline and edges:**
1,700 m
**Overflow edge:** 44 m
**Total water volume:**
ca 12,000 m³
**Flow rate:** 500 m³/h
**Turnover:** 3 days
**Minimum water depth:** 30 cm
**Maximum water depth:** 185 cm
**Cistern volume:**
2,000 m³
**Water treatment:**
Purification biotope
1,900 m² surface area
**Pump power:** 100 kW
**Connected roof area:**
Paved roof 32,000 m²
Green roof ca
12,000 m²
**Annual rainfall:**
530 mm

**Drainage method:**
Evaporation ca
11,570 m³/annum
Toilet flushing ca
10,800 m³/annum
Irrigation ca
1,114 m³/annum
Overflow in Landwehrkanal max. 3l/(s x ha)
**Emergency overflow in canal:** 0,2 %
**Retention volume:**
Water basin 3,100 m³

**Page 50**

Prisma Nürnberg
**Client:**
Karlsruher Lebensversicherung AG
**Water design, glass design:**
Herbert Dreiseitl
**Landscape design:**
Atelier Dreiseitl
**Architect:**
Joachim Eble
Architektur
**Climate simulation:**
Dr. Wilhelm Stahl
**Metalworks:**
Metallatelier Fuchs
**Glassworks:**
Glasgestaltung Dierig
**Planning and design:**
1992 – 1994
**Construction:**
1993 – 1997

**Size:**
Glass house volume
15,000 m³,
glass house area ca
1,400 m²,
external planting
870 m²
**Length:** 110 m
watercourse
**Water surface:** 240 m²
**Total water volume:**
60 m³
**Flow rate:**
1,200 l/min
**Maximum water depth:** 35 cm
**Minimum water depth:** 5 cm
**Cistern volume:**
240 m³ rainwater
storage

**Water treatment:**
190 m² planters,
filters, sedimentation
in cistern;
Purification biotope
50 m² surface area
**Pump power:**
14 kW (2 x 5.5/1 x 3)
**Site area:**
6,000 m²
catchment area
**Residents:** 160
**Impermeable surface:**
100 %
**Annual rainfall:**
675 mm
**Rainfall intensity** $r_{15(1)}$
117.8 l/(s x ha)
**Drainage method:**
Evaporation, infiltration underneath building, reuse (irrigation)
**Soil permeability factor:** $1 \times 10\text{-}4$ m/s
sand subsoil, distance
to groundwater table
$\geq 13$ m
**Infiltration and retention area:**
474 m² under underground parking,
105 m² pond
**Stormwater event:**
10 years

**Page 56**

**Page 58**

**Page 62**

**Page 66**

Art and rainwater
object
Owingen
**Client:**
Gemeinde Owingen
**Water design:**
Herbert Dreiseitl
**Water planning:**
Atelier Dreiseitl
**Architect:**
Huber & Böhler
**Metalworks:**
Metallatelier Fuchs
**Planning and design:**
1998
**Construction:** 1998

**Roof area:**
1,200 m²,
with 40 % green roof
**Annual rainfall:**
780 mm
**Rainfall intensity** $r_{15(1)}$
142 l/(s x ha)
**Drainage method:**
Constructed infiltra-
tion swales
**Soil permeability
factor:**
$\leq 1 \times 10^{-5}$ m/s
**Infiltration and reten-
tion area:** 50 m²
**Stormwater event:**
2 years

Solar City Linz,
Austria
**Client:**
Stadt Linz
**Water design:**
Herbert Dreiseitl
**Landscape design:**
Atelier Dreiseitl
**Architects:**
READ-Gruppe
**Competition:** 1997
**Planning and design:**
1998 – 2001
**Construction:**
1999 – 2005

**Size:** 60 ha
**Settlement area:**
32 ha
**Residents:** 4,500
**Impermeable surface:**
40 %
**Water surface:**
Extension of
Weikerlsee ca
29,000 m²
**Water playgrounds:**
1,000 m²
**Total water volume:**
90,000 m³
**Maximum water
depth:** 400 cm
**Water treatment:**
Purification biotope
200 m² surface area
**Annual rainfall:**
800 mm
**Rainfall intensity** $r_{15(1)}$
125 l/(s x ha)
**Drainage method:**
Drainage and infiltra-
tion (emergency over-
flow > 10 a into
Aumühlbach and
woodland carr along
the Traun)

**Soil permeability
factor:**
Swales $10^{-4}$,
trenches $10^{-2}$
**Infiltration and
retention area:**
9,000 m²
**Stormwater event:**
10 years

Bear enclosure at Zoo
Zürich, Switzerland
**Client:** Zoo Zürich
**Planning of water
system:**
Atelier Dreiseitl
**Landscape design:**
Büro Walter Vetsch
**Planning and design:**
1993 – 1995
**Construction:**
1995 – 1997

**Size:** 4,500 m²
**Length:** 45 m
**Water surface:** 200 m²
**Total water volume:**
300 m³
**Flow rate:**
2,000 l/min
**Maximum turnover
rate:** 2.5 hrs.
**Maximum water
depth:** 150 cm
**Cistern volume:**
15 m³
**Water treatment:**
Purification biotope
105 m² surface area
**Pump power:** 7 kW

Sonnenhausen Estate,
Glonn
**Client:**
K. L. Schweisfurth
Stiftung, Hermanns-
dorfer Landwerk-
stätten
**Water design:**
Herbert Dreiseitl
**Landscape design:**
Atelier Dreiseitl
**Planning and design:**
1987 – 1988
**Construction:** 1989

**Size:**
4,000 m² roof area,
18,000 m² open space
**Length:** 150 m
**Water surface:**
2,000 m²
**Total water volume:**
2,000 m³
**Flow rate:** 100 l/min
**Maximum water
depth:** 130 cm
**Minimum water
depth:** 20 cm
**Water treatment:**
Purification biotope
surface area 200 m²
**Pump power:** 0.75 kW
**Site area:** 22,000 m²
**Residents:** 40
**Impermeable surface:**
30 %
**Annual rainfall:**
850 mm
**Drainage method:**
Surface drains,
retention pond
**Soil permeability
factor:** $1 \times 10^{-6}$
**Infiltration and
retention area:**
200 m²

**Page 68**

Bathing pond in
private garden near
Salzburg
**Water design:**
Herbert Dreiseitl
**Landscape design:**
Atelier Dreiseitl/
Peter Petrich
**Planning and design:**
1984
**Construction:**
1984 – 1988

**Size:** 800 m²
**Water surface:** 400 m²
**Total water volume:**
400 m³
**Flow rate:** 100 l/min
**Maximum Turnover:**
5 days
**Maximum water
depth:** 200 cm
**Minimum water
depth:** 30 cm
**Water treatment:**
Purification biotope
50 m² surface area
**Pump power:**
300 kW

**Page 70**

Coffee Creek Estate,
Indiana, USA
**Client:**
Lake Erie Land
**Water design:**
Atelier Dreiseitl/
Conservation Design
Forum
**Landscape design:**
Conservation Design
Forum
**Architect:**
William McDonough +
Partners
**Contractor:**
Lakeshore Lands-
cape/Gough Construc-
tion
**Planning and design:**
1995 – 1999
**Construction:**
1998 – 2000

**Size:** 260 ha
**Site area:**
2,000 m² designed
watercourse
**Watercourse length:**
60 m
**Width watercourse:**
2 – 3.5 m
**Flow rate:**
3,000 l/min

**Page 76**

EXPO 2000 Hannover
Kronsberg
**Client:**
Stadt Hannover,
Stadtentwässerung
**Water and
Landscape design:**
Atelier Dreiseitl
**General drainage
concept:** ARGE
Dreiseitl/ITWH/IFS
**Planning and design:**
1994 – 1999
**Construction:**
1999 – 2000

**Cistern volume:**
33 m³
**Water treatment:**
Purification biotope
400 m² surface area
**Pump power:**
Solar pumps with ca
1.5 kW each
**Site area:** 130 ha
**Residents:** 15,000
**Impermeable surface:**
80 %
**Annual rainfall:**
750 mm
**Rainfall intensity** $r_{15(1)}$
100 l/(s x ha)
**Drainage method:**
Constructed swales,
retention basins, over-
flow into Rohrgraben
**Soil permeability
factor:** $\leq 1 \times 10^{-6}$ m/s
**Infiltration and
retention area:**
50,000 m²
**Release rate:**
3 l/(s x ha)
**Stormwater event:**
35 years

**Page 80**

Scharnhauser Park,
Ostfildern
**Client:**
Stadt Ostfildern
**Rainwater
management:**
Atelier Dreiseitl
**Urban Design:**
Janson & Wolfrum
**Street planning:**
IB Gmelin
**Planning and design:**
1995 – 1999
**Construction:**
1996 – 2003

**Site area:** 140 ha
**Settlement area:**
70 ha
**Residents:** 9,000
**Impermeable surface:**
60 %
**Annual rainfall:**
700 mm
**Rainfall intensity** $r_{15(1)}$
125 l/(s x ha)
**Drainage method:**
Constructed swales
and trenches, reten-
tion basins, drainage
to Höfelbach and
Krähenbach and
further into Körsch
river
**Soil permeability
factor:** $1 \times 10^{-8}$ m/s
**Infiltration and reten-
tion capacity:**
21,000 m³ swales,
16,000 m³ trenches
**Release rate:**
3 l/(s x ha)
**Stormwater event:**
5 years

**Page 84**

Ecological housing
estate Backumer Tal,
Herten
**Client:**
Veba Immobilien AG
Water design and
**Landscape design:**
Atelier Dreiseitl
**Architects:**
Büro Schaller/
Theodor, Köln
**Circulation plan:**
ITWH
**Green spaces plan:**
Büro Rheims with
H. Geißler
**Planning and design:**
1994 – 1997
**Construction:**
1997 – 2002

**Water surface:** 350 m²
**Maximum water
depth:** 160 cm
**Minimum water
depth:** 10 cm
**Site area:** 13 ha
**Residents:** 1,000
**Impermeable surface:**
30 %
**Annual rainfall:**
780 mm
**Rainfall intensity** $r_{15(1)}$
3,5 l/(s x ha)
**Drainage method:**
Drains and trenches,
infiltration basins,
existing swamp area
and stream
**Soil permeability
factor:** $1 \times 10^{-5}$ m/s
**Infiltration and reten-
tion area:** 5,500 m²
**Stormwater event:**
30 years

**Page 88**

Sewage treatment
plant
**Client:** Treuhand-
verein Wörme: e.V.
**Design:**
Atelier Dreiseitl
**Planning and design:**
1993
**Construction:** 1994

**Size:** 900 m²
**Purification biotope:**
600 m² surface area
**Site area:** 37 ha
**Residents:** 80
**System capacity:**
100 people

**Page 92**

Redesign of Volme
river and town hall
**Client:** Stadt Hagen
**Water design:**
Herbert Dreiseitl
**Landscape design:**
Atelier Dreiseitl
**Architects:**
RKW Architects
**Hydraulics:**
Thomas Nill
**Planning bridge:**
PASD Feldmeier &
Wrede
**Planning and design:**
2000 – 2001
**Construction:**
2001 – 2004

**Length:** Volme 800 m
**Width:** Volme 25 m
**Total water volume:**
Mean rate = 5.67 m³/s
Maximum rate 100 =
249.70 m³/s
**Embankment
redesign:** 12,000 m²

**Page 96**

City Hall, Chicago,
USA
**Client:**
City of Chicago
**Landscape design:**
Atelier Dreiseitl/
Conservation Design
Forum
**Architects:**
William McDonargh &
Partners
**Planning and design:**
1999 – 2000
**Construction:**
2000 – 2001

**Size:**
Roof area ≈3,600 m²,
**planted area:**
2,200 m²

**Page 98**

Redesign Lanferbach,
Gelsenkirchen
**Client:**
Emschergenossen-
schaft
**Water design +
Landscape design:**
Atelier Dreiseitl
**Planning and design:**
1994 – 1998
**Construction:** 1999

**Size:** 32,000 m²
**Length:** 800 m
**Site area:** 12 ha
**Residents:** 1,900
**Annual rainfall:**
775 – 800 mm
**Rainfall intensity** $r_{15(1)}$
115 l/(s x ha)
**Drainage method:**
Constructed swales
and trenches,
infiltration basins
**Soil permeability
factor:** $1 \times 10^{-5}$ m/s
**Infiltration and
retention area:**
4,000 m²
**Release rate:**
Mean rate = 7.5 l/s
Maximum rate =
76.1 l/s

**Page 102**

Estate »Hameau de la
Fontaine« Echallens,
Switzerland
**Client:**
Theiler & Partner,
Murten
**Water design and
Landscape design:**
Atelier Dreiseitl
**Architects:**
Theiler & Partner
**Planning and design:**
1981 – 1984
**Construction:**
1982 – 1986

**Size:** 50,000 m²
**Length:** 80 m perma-
nent watercourses
**Water surface:** 350 m²
**Total water volume:**
250 m³
**Flow rate:** 300 l/min
**Maximum water
depth:** 120 cm pond
**Minimum water
depth:** 5 cm channel
**Cistern volume:** 5 m³
**Water treatment:**
Purification biotope
100 m² surface area
**Pump power:** 0.75 kW
**Roof area:** 2,200 m²
**Residents:** 250
**Impermeable surface:**
60 %
**Annual rainfall:**
850 mm
**Drainage method:**
Surface drains, reten-
tion pond, drainage
into stream

| Page 104 | Page 108 | Page 112 | Page 114 | Page 118 |
|---|---|---|---|---|

**Business park Krems-Ost, Austria**
**Client:**
Magistrat der Stadt Krems
**Rainwater management:**
Atelier Dreiseitl
**Street planning:**
IB Spindelberger
**Planning and design:**
1995 – 1996
**Construction:**
1996 – 1998

**Site area:**
330,000 m²
**Impermeable surface in business park:**
80 – 90 %
**Annual rainfall:**
800 mm
**Rainfall intensity** $r_{15(1)}$
83 l/(s x ha)
**Drainage method:**
Infiltration swales and basins
**Soil permeability factor:** $1 \times 10^{-3}$ m/s
**Infiltration and retention area:**
3,280 m²
**Stormwater event:**
5 years

**BUGA 97 Phenomena in cooling tower**
**Client:**
Bundesgartenschau 97 GmbH
**Artistic concept:**
Herbert Dreiseitl
**Design:**
Atelier Dreiseitl
**Architects:**
PASD Feldmeier & Wrede
**Structural engineers:**
IPP Polonyi & Partner
**Consultants:**
Institut für Strömungswissenschaften, FH Konstanz, Max Planck Institut Göttingen
**Planning and design:**
1994 – 1996
**Construction:** 1997

**Tower height:** 28 m
**Visitor platform:**
ca 300 m²
**Flow rate:**
200 m³/hr. (maximum)
**Pump power:** 5 kW

**Teaching centre Marquart, Burgberg**
**Client:** Lehrstätte für Reflexionsarbeit am Fuß
**Water design:**
Herbert Dreiseitl
**Landscape design:**
Atelier Dreiseitl
**Planning and design:**
1989
**Construction:**1990

**Size:** 200 m²
**Length:** 25 m
**Water surface:** 20 m²
**Flow rate:** 100 l/min
**Maximum water depth:** 100 cm
**Cistern volume:** 2 m³
**Water treatment:**
Purification biotope
**Pump power:** 0.55 kW

**Landing pier Immenstaad am Bodensee**
**Client:**
Gemeinde Immenstaad
**Water design:**
Herbert Dreiseitl
**Landscape design:**
Wolfgang Holste
**Planning and design:**
1990
**Construction:** 1991

**Flow rate:** 600 l/min
**System:** pumped lake water
**Pump power:** 0.9 kW

**documenta urbana**
**Client:**
Neue Heimat Südwest, Frankfurt
**Water design:**
Atelier Dreiseitl
**Landscape design:**
Raimund Herms
**Planning and design:**
1981 – 1983
**Construction:** 1984

**Water surface:** 800 m²
**Embankment Length:**
150 m
**Total water volume:**
250 m³
**Flow rate:** 180 l/min
**Maximum water depth:** 70 cm
**Minimum water depth:** 20 cm
**Water treatment:**
Purification biotope
**Pump power:** 0.5 kW
**Site area:** 15,000 m²
**Residents:**
124 apartments
**Impermeable surface:**
30 %
**Annual rainfall:**
800 mm
**Rainfall intensity** $r_{15(1)}$
300 l/(s x ha)
**Drainage method:**
Open drains, retention pond
**Infiltration and retention area:**
500 m²

**Page 120**

EXPO 2000 Wasser-
themen Bad Pyrmont
**Client:**
Stadt Bad Pyrmont
**Water design:**
Herbert Dreiseitl
**Landscape design:**
Atelier Dreiseitl
**Architects:**
Architekturbüro
Brandstetter
**Sound concept main
avenue:**
Andres Bosshard
**Light and sound
objects main avenue:**
Metallatelier Fuchs
**Planning and design:**
1998 – 1999
**Construction:**
1999 – 2000

**Size of park at
»Dunsthöhle«:**
5,000 m²
**Length of sound
installation:**
250 m main avenue

**Page 128**

EXPO 2000 Water
traces Hann. Münden
**Client:**
Stadt Hann. Münden
**Water design:**
»Szene«
Herbert Dreiseitl
**Planning and design:**
Atelier Dreiseitl
**Planning of squares:**
BSF, Ulrich Franke
**Artists:**
»Hoch« Diether Heisig,
Uli Westerfrölke (air)
»Serie Speier« Jens
and Hans-Werner
Kalkmann
»Tief und Streuung«
Wolfgang
Rossdeutscher
»Klang, Dramaturgie«
Andres Bosshard
**Water carpet and
sound/light steles
(steel):**
Metallatelier Fuchs
**Glass:**
Glasgestaltung Dierig
**Planning and design:**
1997 – 1999
**Construction:**
1999 – 2000

**Size »Szene«:**
ca 1,100 m²
**Water surface:** 180 m²
**Flow rate:** 400 l/min
**Water depth:** 4 cm
**Cistern volume:** 35 m³
**Water treatment:**
Reversible automatic
sandfilter
**Pump power:**
10.5 kW total
**Catchment area:**
Church, townhall
2,000 m²

**Lighting:**
50 m fibre optics
cables

**Page 132**

Interior courtyard
Nicolaus-Cusanus-
Haus, Stuttgart
**Client:**
Baugemeinschaft
Birkach GBR
**Water design:**
Herbert Dreiseitl
**Landscape design:**
Atelier Dreiseitl/
G. Bockemühl
**Architects:**
Bockemühl, Weller
und Partner
**Planning and design:**
1987 – 1990
**Construction:**
1990 – 1991

**Size:** 800 m²
**Water surface:** 70 m²
**Flow rate:** 100 l/min
**Water depth basin:**
25 cm
**Water treatment:**
Self-regulating
macro-filter
**Pump power:** 0.55 kW

**Page 136**

Schafbrühl estate,
Tübingen
**Client:**
Karlsruher Lebens-
versicherung AG
**Water design:**
Herbert Dreiseitl
**Landscape design:**
Christof Harms/
Herbert Dreiseitl
**Architects:**
Eble + Sambeth,
Häfele, Oed
**Planning and design:**
1984 – 1985
**Construction:** 1986

**Watercourse length:**
150 m
**Water surface:** 120 m²
**Total water volume:**
80 m³
**Flow rate:** 200 l/min.
**Maximum water
depth:** 150 cm pond
**Cistern volume:**
8.6 m³
**Water treatment:**
Pre-filter, mud trap,
pond with purification
biotope, 120 m²
surface area
**Pump power:** 0.75 kW
**Site area:** 13,000 m²
**Residents:** 120
**Impermeable surface:**
65 %
**Drainage method:**
Surface drains,
retention pond,
overflow into canal

**Page 138**

**Page 140**

Fountain for the blind,
Duft- und Tastgarten
LGS 1980 Ulm
**Client:**
Gartenbaumt Ulm
**Water design:**
Herbert Dreiseitl
**Landscape design:**
Planungsgruppe
Eppinger & Schmid
**Planning and design:**
1979
**Construction:**
1979 – 1980

**Size:** square 45 m², 
fountain 15 m²
**Flow rate:** 700 l/min
**Cistern volume:**
12 m³
**Water treatment:**
Mechanical filter

Water playground
LGS 92, Pforzheim
**Client:**
Stadt Pforzheim
**Water design:**
Herbert Dreiseitl
**Landscape design:**
Atelier Dreiseitl
**Planning and design:**
1988 – 1989
**Construction:**
1990 – 1991

**Size:** 4,000 m²
**Water surface:** 300 m²
**System:** 80 %
circulation with 20 %
permanent introduc-
tion of fresh water
**Total water volume:**
60 m³
**Flow rate:**
150 – 300 l/min,
circulation partially
manual

# List of works

**1980**: Berlin/
school yard biotope

**1980**: Ulm
LGS '80/fountain
for the blind
**Client**: Stadt Ulm

**1980**: Oslo (N)/
school yard design
Steinerskolen
**Client**: private

**1980**: Dribergen (NL)
Vrije Hogeschool/
water feature
**Client**:
Vrije Hogeschool

**1980**: Utrecht (NL)/
research facility
Warmonderhof
**Client**: private

**1981**: München/
fountain at Wohnhof
Cosima

**1981**: Koblenz/
retention pond, watercourse
**Client**:
AWK

**1981**: Schwenningen/
fountain in courtyard
of vocational school
**Client**: LGS Reutlingen
1984 GmbH

**1981**: Hepsisau/
flowform cascade
**Client**:
Heimsonderschule Hepsisau

**1981**: Engelberg/
school yard biotope
**Client**:
Waldorfschule Engelberg

**1981**: Trubschachen (CH)/
sewage treatment plant
**Client**:
Bergbauernhof

**1981**: Witten-Annen/
park with water feature
**Client**:
Lehrerseminar Witten-Annen

**1981**: Überlingen/
flowform cascade
**Client**: Freie Waldorfschule
Rengoldshausen

**1982**: Gaienhofen/
school yard design and water
feature
**Client**: Grund- und Haupt-
schule Gaienhofen

**1982**: Wädenswil (CH)/
pond and watercourse
**Client**:
Kinderheim Bühl

**1982**: Perceval St. Prex
(CH)/water garden
**Client**:
Camphill Perceval

**1982**: Nürnberg/
flowform cascade
**Client**:
Ev. Altenheim Zürndorf

**1983**: Kassel
documenta urbana/
bowl cascade
**Client**:
Neue Heimat Nordhessen

**1983**: Herten/
flowform cascade
**Client**:
Fa. Schweißfurt

**1983**: Berlin/
flowform cascade
Kunstgewerbemuseum
**Client**:
Kunstgewerbemuseum

**1983**: Würrenlos (CH)/
private garden
**Client**: private

**1984**: Darmstadt/
flowform feature
**Client**:
Software AG Darmstadt

**1984**: Reutlingen LGS '84/
fountain
**Client**:
LGS Reutlingen
1984 GmbH

**1984**: Stuttgart/
Pfarrgarten Jagststraße
**Client**: TBA Stuttgart

**1984:** Berlin/
school yard design
Hoverschule Berlin
**Client:** Senat Berlin

**1984:** Kopenhagen (DK)/
private garden
**Client:** private

**1984:** Amsterdam (NL)/
fountain Floriade

**1985:** Tübingen
Schafbrühl/Virbella
cascades and rainwater
management
**Client:** Karlsruher
Lebensversicherung

**1985:** Stuttgart/
Fountainhaus Jagdstraße
**Client:**
TBA Stuttgart

**1985:** Witten-Annen/
private garden Fischer
**Client:** Fischer

**1985:** Osnabrück/
water feature with cascade
**Client:**
Naturwissenschaftliches
Museum

**1985:** Frankfurt am Main/
cascade at old people's
home

**1985:** Föhrenbühl/
water feature
Heimsonderschule
**Client:** Heimsonderschule
Föhrenbühl

**1985:** Löffingen/
private garden
**Client:** private

**1985:** Ohmenhausen/
fountain
**Client:** Gemeinde
Ohmenhausen

**1985:** Frankfurt am Main/
private roof garden
**Client:** private

**1986:** Echallens (CH)
Estate »Hameau de la
Fontaine«/landscape design
and rainwater management
**Client:** Architekturbüro
Theiler + Partner

**1986:** Remmingsheim/
fountain
**Client:**
Gemeinde Remmingsheim

**1986:** Rio Pradillo (E)/
sewage treatment plant
**Client:** private

**1987:** Vaerloese (DK)/
garden with flowforms
**Client:** private

**1987:** Heidenheim
Waldorfschule/water
feature in school yard
**Client:**
Freie Waldorfschule
Heidenheim

**1987:** Düsseldorf
BUGA '87/water playground
**Client:** Bundesgartenschau
1987 GmbH

**1987:** Baienfurt /
fountain, potable water
sculpture, green island
**Client:**
Gemeinde Baienfurt

**1988:** Kirchberg/
olympia cascade
in private garden
**Client:** private

**1988:** Zuffenhausen/
landscape design and
rainwater management
**Client:**
Siedlungswerk Stuttgart
GmbH

**1988:** Glonn
Gut Sonnenhausen/
open spaces
**Client:** Hermannsdorfer
Landwerkstätten

**1988:** Gänserndorf (A)
Siedlung Gärtnerhof/
rainwater management
**Client:**
Helmut Warter & Co GmbH

**1988:** Murten (CH)
Theiler/fountain sculpture
**Client:** AB Theiler+Partner

**1988:** Bern (CH)
Estate «Im Park«
Ittigen/fountain, water
feature and landscape design
**Client:**
Berner Lebensversicherungs-
Gesellschaft

**1988:** Viernheim/
design Town Hall Square
**Client:**
Stadt Viernheim

**1988:** Fellbach/
fountain
**Client:** Fa. Maier

**1988:** Fellbach/
fountain at kindergarten
Fellbach
**Client:**
Kindergarten Fellbach

**1988:** Lausanne (CH)/
retention pond for Gärtnerei
La Branche
**Client:** private

**1989:** Überlingen/
fountain at vocational school
**Client:** Landratsamt

**1989:** Glonn
Gut Hermannsdorf/
water management
**Client:**
Hermannsdorfer
Landwerkstätten

**1989:** Salzburg (A)/
swimming pond
**Client:** private

**1989:** Stadt Krems (A)/
water management
**Client:** Magistrat
der Stadt Krems

**1989:** Billafingen/
natural pond
**Client:** private

**1989:** Urnau/
sewage treatment plant
at summer camp Benistobel
**Client:** Katholische
Erzdiözese Rottenburg

**1989:** Wien (A)/
interior fountain at Teestube
Dreiklang
**Client:** private

**1989:** Überlingen/
fountain and square design
at post office
**Client:**
Deutsche Bundespost

**1990:** Murrhardt/
fountain
**Client:**
Stadt Murrhardt

**1990:** Zutphen (NL)
Ijsselpromenade/water and
play object, square design
**Client:** Stiftung »WEL«

**1990:** Montezillon (CH)
L'Aubier/musical fountain
and rainwater management
**Client:** L'Aubier

**1990:** Überlingen
Burgberg/rainwater
management
**Client:** private

**1990:** Berlin/
cascade Tempelhof
**Client:** Senat Berlin

**1990:** Ravensburg/
light design in
administration building
**Client:**
Deutsche Bundespost

**1990:** Ravensburg/
landscape design
**Client:**
Deutsche Bundespost

**1990:** Darmstadt/
fountain at kindergarten
Darmstadt
**Client:**
Stadt Darmstadt

**1990:** Heiligenberg
Schlosscafe Neyer
**Client:** Neyer

**1990:** Berlin/
Max-Eyth-Park
**Client:**
Senat Berlin

**1991:** Immenstaad/
water feature at
landing pier
**Client:** Gemeinde
Immenstaad

**1991**: Heilbronn/
Cäcilien fountain/refurbish-
ment and new design
**Client**:
Stadt Heilbronn

**1991**: Ulm
Fa. Wilken/landscape design
**Client**: Wilken
Software GmbH

**1991**: Königsfeld/
private garden with
water feature
**Client**:
Lehrstätte Marquardt

**1991**: Furtwangen/
rainwater concept
Kussenhof estate
**Client**:
Stadt Furtwangen

**1991**: Hausach/
Fountain
**Client**: private

**1991**: Bern-Ittigen (CH)/
private garden
**Client**: private

**1991**: Hattersheim/
water staircase, marketplace
design, watercourse
**Client**:
Stadt Hattersheim

**1992**: Pforzheim
LGS '92/water
playground
**Client**:
LGS Pforzheim 92 GmbH

**1992**: Karlsruhe
Private garden/
flowform bowls
**Client**: private

**1992**: Salem/
sewage treatment plant
Hagenweilerhof
**Client**: private

**1992**: Euskirchen/
swimming pool Euskirchen
**Client**:
Stadt Euskirchen

**1992**: Marutendorf/
sewage treatment plant
Gut Marutendorf
**Client**: private

**1993**: Viernheim
Schmittsberg/rainwater
management
**Client**:
Stadt Viernheim

**1993**: Stuttgart
Nicolaus-Cusanus-Haus/
interior courtyard with
watercourses
**Client**: Baugemeinschaft
Birkach GmbH

**1993**: Stuttgart
Forum 3/flowform-Fountain
im Innenhof

**1993**: Wiesneck
Husemann-Klinik/
water source
**Client**: Friedrich-Husemann-
Klinik

**1993**: Freiburg
Heliotrop/water concept
**Client**: Rolf Disch

**1993**: Waiblingen/
water feature in interior
courtyard of pharmacy
**Client**: Sonnen-
apotheke Waiblingen

**1993**: Saffig
Brüderkrankenhaus/
flowform cascade
**Client**:
Brüderkrankenhaus Saffig

**1993**: Bulle (CH)
Estate »En Dardens«/
water object in parking
garage
**Client**: Architekturbüro
Theiler+Partner

**1994**: »De Bol«,
Insel Texel (NL)
De Witteberg/water
playground
**Client**: private

**1994**: Duderstadt
LNS'94/water playground
**Client**: Natur im Städtebau,
Duderstadt 94 GmbH

1994: Herten
Backumer Tal/open space
and rainwater concept
Client:
Veba Immobilien

1994: Bad Dürrheim
LGS '94/garden and
water design
Client: LGS'94 GmbH

1994: Bad Boll
Wala/fountain object
in production hall
Client:
Wala-Heilmittel GmbH

1994: Steißlingen
Baumschule Ammann/
refurbishment of sales
and exhibition area
Client:
Baumschule Ammann

1994: Buchholz
Hofgemeinschaft
Wörme/sewage
treatment plant
Client: Treuhandverein
Wörme e.V.

1994: Düsseldorf
Lennéschule/refurbishment
of school yard, landscape
and water design
Client:
LHPTS, Düsseldorf

1994: Hannover
Kronsberg/feasibility
study
Client: Stadt Hannover

1994: Münsingen/
drainage concept
Client: STEG Stadt-
entwicklung Südwest

1994: Ebratsweiler/
sewage treatment
plant van Dijk
Client: private

1994: Berlin/
swimming pool
Zingster Straße
Client: Senat Berlin

1994: Gelsenkirchen
Schüngelberg estate
Client:
Stadt Gelsenkirchen

1994: Wunsiedel/
cascade
Client: private

1994: Schienen/
sewage treatment plant
Client: private

1995: Ostfildern
LGS 2002/water
management of estate
Client:
Stadt Ostfildern

1995: Solingen
Börkhauser Feld/
water management
Client:
Spar & Bauverein Solingen

1995: Ostfildern
Scharnhauser Park/study,
rainwater concept, drainage
management
Client:
Stadt Ostfildern

1995: Hohnstein/
water study
Client:
Archi Nova Hohnstein GmbH

1995: Ostrach
Im Alten Spitz III/green
spaces plan and stormwater
concept
Client:
Gemeinde Ostrach

1995: Heiligenberg
Heimsonderschule
Föhrenbühl/design for
a therapeutic bath
Client: Heimsonderschule
Föhrenbühl

1995: Owingen/
fountain
Client: Bürgermeisteramt
Owingen

1995: Weil der Stadt/
cascade
Client: private

1996: Halle
Tornau-Mötzlich/drainage
study
Client: HWA,
Hallesche Wasser und
Abwasser GmbH

1996: Hannover
Kronsberg/feasibility study,
rainwater concept
Client: LHS Hannover

1996: Wald
Sägen-Weiher/
zoning plan
Client: URBSCHAT/
Wohn- und Gewerbebau
GmbH

1996: Linz (A)
Solar City Pichling/land-
scape concept, stormwater
management
Client: Stadt Linz

1996: Wisconsin (USA)
East Troy/landscape and
water design
Client: private

1997: Linz (A)
Gartenhof Loidt/
water purification
Client: Arbeitsgemeinschaft
für anthroposophisches
Heilwesen

1997: VS-Villingen
Schilterhäusle II/
drainage plan
Client: TDA VS

1997: Zürich (CH)
Zoo/water concept
for bear enclosure
Client: Zoo Zürich

**1997:** Hagenweilerhof/
sewage treatment plant
**Client:** private

**1997:** Kaiserslautern
Barbarossa-Business-
Park/drainage concept
**Client:** Stadtentwässerung
Kaiserslautern

**1997:** Nürnberg
Gostenhof/design of interior
courtyard, climate control
by water walls
**Client:** Karlsruher
Lebensversicherung

**1997:** Gelsenkirchen
BUGA '97/water phenomena
in cooling tower
**Client:** BUGA '97

**1997:** Gelsenkirchen
Eingang Nord BUGA '97/
water ramp and water
feature with fountain
**Client:**
BUGA '97 GmbH

**1998:** Mannheim
Wallstadt-Nord/II. BA/
open spaces and stormwater
concept
**Client:**
SÜBA Consult, Abtlg. GEV

**1998:** Bad Cannstatt
DRK Krankenhaus/
fountain in hospital foyer
**Client:**
DRK Krankenhaus

**1998:** Korntal
Brüdergemeinde/fountain
in community garden
**Client:** Brüdergemeinde
Korntal

**1998:** Wuppertal
Klippe/open spaces
and drainage concept
**Client:** GWG

**1998:** Cressia (F)
Les Serans/rainwater
concept for guesthouse
**Client:** private

**1998:** Bad Boll/
flowform cascade
**Client:** private

**1998:** Göttingen
Zietenkaserne/study
of rainwater concept
**Client:**
Baudezernat Stadt Göttingen

**1998:** Heidenheim/
water design in
private garden
**Client:** private

**1998:** Bitterfeld
Wasserwerk/feasibility study
for waterworks conversion
**Client:** EXPO 2000
Sachsen-Anhalt GmbH

**1998:** Castrop Rauxel/
study for the use
of rainwater
**Client:** IBA Emscher
Park GmbH

**1998:** Kaiserslautern
PRE-Park-Holtzendorff/
rainwater concept
**Client:**
WVE Westpfälzische Ver-
und Entsorgungs GmbH

**1998:** Bad Pyrmont/
water themes,
water study
**Client:**
Stadt Bad Pyrmont

**1998:** Kaiserslautern
»Am Obergarten«
Morlautern/rainwater
concept
**Client:** Stadtentwässerung
Kaiserslautern

**1998:** Glonn/
general drainage plan
**Client:** GKF
Gesellschaft für kommunale
Fachdienste Gbr

**1998:** Hamm
Maximilianpark/design
concept for art installation
**Client:**
Maximilianpark GmbH

**1998:** Lugano (CH )
Schweizer Bankgesell-
schaft/pond design,
water technology
**Client:** INTEP AG

**1998:** Kreuzlingen (CH)/
swimming pond
**Client:** private

**1998:** Owingen/
rainwater concept
with art object for school
**Client:**
Gemeinde Owingen

**1999:** Therwil (CH)/
rainwater concept,
quality management
for several estates
**Client:**
Gemeinde Therwil

**1999:** Berlin
Potsdamer Platz/design,
planning of urban water
basins
**Client:** Stadt Berlin/
Debis Immobilien

**1999:** Gelsenkirchen
Lanferbach/semi-natural
redesign of wastewater-
course
**Client:**
Emschergenossenschaft

**1999:** Hannover
Stadtteil Kronsberg/
rainwater concept, retention
areas as city park
**Client:**
Stadtentwässerung
Hannover

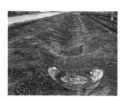

**1999:** Stuttgart
SSB Stuttgarter Straßen-
bahnen/drainage of city
train track area
**Client:** SSB AG

**1999:** Gummersbach/
watercourse, square
and water design
**Client:**
Stadt Gummersbach

**1999:** Gummersbach
Sparkasse/fountain,
glass art, climate control
**Client:**
Sparkasse Gummersbach

**1999:** Harlemville,
New York (USA)/
landscape and water
design
**Client:** RSEFA

**1999:** Asperg
Lange Äcker/landscape
design, drainage and
rainwater concept
**Client:** Strenger Bauen
und Wohnen GmbH

**1999:** Warstein/
study of rainwater
in industrial estates
**Client:** Ministerium für
Umwelt, Raumordnung und
Landwirtschaft (NRW)

**1999:** Wiesbaden/
farmstead for children
**Client:**
Verein Kinderbauernhof e.V.

**1999:** Herne-Sodingen
Akademie/water design for
square and glass building
**Client:** EMC, Entwicklungsgesellschaft Mont Cenis

**1999:** Berlin
Design of interior courtyard
**Client:** private

**1999:** Sipplingen
Private garden
**Client:** private

**1999:** Überlingen
St. Leonhard park,
art objects
**Client:**
NABU

**1999:** Unterbach
Sewage treatment plant
**Client:** private

**2000:** Hann. Münden
EXPO 2000
Wasserspuren/square and
water design,
technical concept
**Client:**
Stadt Hann. Münden

**2000:** Geldern
Marketplace/water design
**Client:**
Stadt Geldern

**2000:** Heidelberg
Print-Media-Academy/
design study, water installation in auditorium
**Client:** Heidelberger Druck-
maschinen AG

**2000:** Erftstadt/
circulation and purification
for Gorsch swimming pond
**Client:** private

**2000:** Karlsruhe
Kronenplatz/square
and water design
**Client:**
Stadt Karlsruhe

**2000:** Villingen-
Schwenningen/
fountain and redesign for
natural stream at cemetary
**Client:** Stadt
Villingen-Schwenningen

**2000:** Schramberg
Schoren Süd/water
management and land-
scape design for estate
**Client:**
Stadt Schramberg

**2000:** Hagen/
staircase at townhall, open
spaces and water design
**Client:** Stadt Hagen

**2000:** Davenport (USA)/
Mississippi riverfront concept
workshop, pre-design
**Client:** River Action

**2000:** Coffee Creek (USA)/
open space and water design

**2000:** Chicago (USA)
Chicago City Hall/
roof garden
**Client:** private

**2000:** Sydney (AU)
Kogarah Town Square/town
square design, stormwater
management
**Client:** Kogarah Council

**2000:** Köln/
design study for water features, Gerling-Neubau Köln
**Client:**
Gerling-Konzern Köln

**2000:** Queens,
New York (USA)/
Queens Botanical Garden,
masterplan concept
**Client:** Queens Botanical
Garden

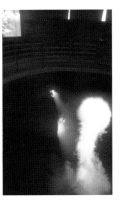

**2000:** Bad Pyrmont
EXPO 2000/exhibition
»WasserLeben«
**Client:**
Stadt Bad Pyrmont

**2000:** Bad Pyrmont/
sound installation
Hauptallee
**Client:**
Stadt Bad Pyrmont

**2000:** New York,
New York (USA)/
Green Administration
Building, landscape
concept and design
**Client:**
City of New York

# The authors

**Herbert Dreiseitl,** born in 1955, is a sculptor, water artist and interdisciplinary planner. After his studies, he set up his office, Atelier Dreiseitl, in Überlingen on Lake Constance in 1980. He has realized numerous projects in the fields of urban hydrology, water design, leisure planning, housing estate drainage etc.

**Prof. Wolfgang Geiger** is one of the few experts in natural water management. He is head of the Department of Water Management at the Universität Gesamthochschule in Essen, Faculty of Building.

**Dieter Grau,** born in 1963, studied landscape design in Nürtingen. He has worked for Atelier Dreiseitl since 1994, where he became head of the Open Space and Project Planning Department in 1996.

**Prof. Detlev Ipsen** teaches in the Department of Planning Method and Empirical Planning Research at the Gesamthochschule in Kassel, faculty of Urban and Regional Sociology. Editor of the publication »Wasserkultur – Beiträge zu einer nachhaltigen Stadtentwicklung«, Berlin, 1998.

**Stefan Leppert,** born in 1959, bank employee, gardener, engineering diploma in landscape architecture, specialist editor for the magazine »Garten + Landschaft« in Munich, owner of the 'phase_neun« editorial office in Münster since spring 2001.

**Prof. Karl H. C. Ludwig,** born in 1952, studied landscape architecture in Berlin and Vienna. He has been a free-lance landscape architect in Munich since 1985, numerous publications on the subject of urban green spaces and the home environment. Professor of »Constructive Design in Open Space Planning« at the Fachhochschule in Nürtingen since 1991.

**Wolfram Schwenk** is a hydrobiologist and leading member of the private Institute of Flow Sciences in Herrischried in the southern Black Forest. The institute is known for Theodor Schwenk's book »Sensitive Chaos« and is devoted to water research.

**Robert Woodward,** born in 1923 in Australia, studied architecture and landscape architecture in Sydney, where he directs his own water design office.

Andreas Arnold
**Pages:** 28df, 32d

Andreas Bockemühl
**Pages:** 62abc, 63, 64, 65ab, 88abcde, 90c, 115ab, 147bc, 148a

Andreas Böhmer
**Page:** 131a

Conservation Design Forum
**Pages:** 70ab, 71bcd

Debis Immobilien
**Page:** 153bc

Herbert Dreiseitl
**Pages:** Cover, 14abcd, 15, 16abc, 18abcd, 19, 20abcd, 21ab, 22ab, 24bc, 25, 26abcde, 27, 28abce, 29, 31abcde, 32bc, 33, 36ab, 37, 39abcde, 44abc-defg, 45, 46ae, 48abcdfg, 49, 54e, 60, 66abc, 67, 68abc, 69, 71a, 76d, 77a, 78ab, 80a, 82abcdfgh, 89, 90ab, 92ab, 96abc, 97a, 99b, 102abcde, 103, 108abcde, 109, 112abcd, 113, 114, 115c, 116abcde, 117, 118abcd, 119, 120cdef, 129, 130abc, 132, 133abcd, 134abc, 136abcde, 137a, 138abcd, 139, 140, 141abcdef, 144abc, 145abcde, 146abc, 147a, 148bc, 148bc, 150abcdef, 151abc, 152abcde, 153a, 154, 155, 174, 176

Siegfried J. Gragnato
**Pages:** 50, 51a, 55

Dieter Grau
**Pages:** 48e, 53c, 56, 57abcd, 76abc, 77b, 84abcd, 85, 86abc, 98, 99acde, 100abcd, 101, 120ab, 121, 122bc, 123ab, 62abc, 31ce

Werner Hannappel
**Page:** 110abcd

Hanuschke & Schneider
**Pages:** 128c, 131b

Thomas Hoffmann
**Pages:** 51b, 53a, 82e, 83, 104abc, 105abc

Brant Kilber
**Pages:** Cover back, 32a, 53b, 54abcd, 128abd, 149b

Berner Leben
**Pages:** 36c, 38b

Magistrat Linz
**Pages:** 58ab, 61

Entwicklungsgesellschaft
Mont-Cenis mbH
**Pages:** 23, 24a

Jens Pfisterer
**Page:** 30

Dominik Rottweiler
**Pages:** 122ad, 130d

3 D Visual
**Pages:** 46bc, 52ab

Harald Wegener
**Page:** 130e

# Illustration credits

| a | b | c |
| d | e | f |
| g | h | i |

Project texts: Stefan Leppert
Graphic design: Michael Kimmerle, Stuttgart
Translation into English: Michael Robinson

This book is also available in a German language
edition. (ISBN 3-7643-6508-0)

A CIP catalogue record for this book is available
from the Library of Congress, Washington D.C., USA

Deutsche Bibliothek Cataloging-in-Publication Data

Waterscapes – planning, building and designing
with water/ed. by Herbert Dreiseitl ...
[Transl. into Engl.: Michael Robinson]. –
Basel; Berlin; Boston: Birkhäuser, 2001
        Dt. Ausg. u.d.T.: Waterscapes - Bauen, Planen
        und Gestalten mit Wasser
ISBN 3-7643-6410-6

©2001 Birkhäuser – Publishers for Architecture,
P.O. Box 133, CH-4010 Basel, Switzerland
A member of the BertelsmannSpringer
Publishing Group
Printed on acid-free paper produced
from chlorine-free pulp. TCF ∞

Printed in Germany
ISBN 3-7643-6410-6

9 8 7 6 5 4 3 2

http://www.birkhauser.ch